the Wild Cats

the Wild Cats

by Edward R. Ricciuti

A Ridge Press Book

Windward

Editor-in-Chief: Jerry Mason
Editor: Adolph Suehsdorf
Art Director: Harry Brocke
Associate Editor: Ronne Peltzman
Associate Editor: Marta Hallett
Art Associate: Nancy Mack
Art Associate: Liney Li
Art Production: Doris Mullane
Picture Editor: Marion Geisinger
Production Consultant: Arthur Gubernick

Windward
an imprint owned by W. H. Smith & Son Ltd.
Registered number 737811 England
Trading as   WHS Distributors
             Euston Street
             Freemen's Common
             Aylestone Road
             Leicester LE2 7SS
All rights reserved
ISBN 07112 0010 6

Printed and bound in the Netherlands
by Smeets Offset, Weert.

To John Hax

Contents

Sleek and strong, marvels of controlled power, grace, and beauty, the wild cats of the world are the quintessential predators. Whether large or small, all cats possess a combination of qualities that make them the superb hunters they are. Chief among these are astonishing stealth, remarkable agility, and muscles that are steely but wondrously supple. Since prehistoric times, these qualities have inspired in humans awe, envy, and sometimes chilling fear.

There are strong indications that leopards regularly preyed on the ancient ancestors of modern man in Africa, much as the spotted cats hunt baboons there today. Later peoples, living near the end of the glacial epoch, depicted cats of various types on the walls of caves in Europe. On one cave wall in the Dordogne region of France, an ancient artist etched a creature with an elongated head and neck, erect, pointed ears, and a broad face—an animal that could pass for a modern bobcat or even a house cat. In Les Combarelles, another cave in the same region, there is a portrait of an even more imposing beast, the great cave lion that prowled Europe through much of the ice age.

The cave lion has vanished, but many of the great cats of today are no less imposing, and felines still have the power to excite the human imagination. This book focuses on the wild cats, especially those that are large and regal, presenting an intimate view of these creatures that represent nature at its grandest. The wild cats belong to the natural world, and while some have adapted their ways to the presence of humans, as a group they truly flourish only where nature is in balance—not necessarily pristine, but not devastated by human encroachment.

Wild cats are native to every continent except Australia and Antarctica. Within this immense area, they have adapted to a tremendous range of environments, demonstrating how, through evolutionary change, one basic type of animal has radiated into many specialized varieties. Cats of one sort or another can be found at the fringes of the Arctic; on the world's highest mountains; on broad plains; in dense swampland; on sizzling, arid deserts; in wintry conifer forests; in dank, shadowy jungles; and on foggy moorlands. Some of these cats are commonly seen by human eyes. Others are so secretive and inhabit haunts so remote from human settlements that they are almost never glimpsed by people.

Wild cats have existed for millions of years, although the earliest forms were quite different in their biological characteristics from most modern felines. The lines by which the cats evolved are not entirely clear, and there is disagreement among scientists about the feline family tree. Research in this area is proceeding vigorously, especially at such institutions as the American Museum of Natural History in New York City.

Looking very much like the legendary "king of beasts," a male lion gazes placidly through the grass on the plains of Tanzania. Like the other wild cats, the lion is powerful yet graceful, a keen hunter and fearsome adversary.

9

Giving the lie to the idea that cats despise water, two tigers play in a jungle river. Tigers are especially fond of water and often soak just to cool off. Although most tigers today inhabit the tropics, the species originated in northern Asia.

Other scientists have turned their attention to the living cats, in an effort to learn more about the way they live and how they relate to their environment. Foremost among the researchers who have studied the wild cats in nature is George B. Schaller of the New York Zoological Society. His field studies of wild cats are considered classics because of his diligent attention to details and because of the length of time devoted to each study—usually several years per project. Schaller has closely observed the lion and the cheetah in Africa, the tiger in India, and the snow leopard in the high mountains of Asia. At this writing, he is beginning an investigation of the jaguar in South America.

To truly probe the lives of cats in the wild demands not only an interest in the animals· and some understanding of their biology, but also extraordinary physical stamina, a willingness to put up with hardship and deprivation, and occasionally great courage—not so much because the cats are dangerous, but because the environment often is hazardous. To observe the snow leopard in its native surroundings, for example, one must make his or her way through treacherous mountains in ice, snow, and pounding winds—conditions that could end of the life of someone not prepared to cope with them.

The need to learn more about the wild cats, especially the larger ones, is of critical importance today, because many

10

With its head only half above water, a jaguar cruises a tropical waterway. This cat often goes into the water after prey, including some of the largest freshwater fishes in the world.

of these creatures are vanishing. Some of the cats are seriously endangered, and others, such as the Asian cheetah and lion, are all but extinct. Some races of tiger have disappeared just within the last few generations. If the wild cats are to be saved, we must understand their environmental needs and how they are affected by human activities.

Such knowledge is critical because the wild cats are no longer the masters of their environment. The stealth, strength, and cunning they have acquired over millions of years of evolution are no longer sufficient to guarantee their survival. No amount of skill at stalking and bringing down prey can help a cat when the environment that supports the prey has been destroyed. The ability to move furtively through cover is virtually useless when there is no place left to hide. Indeed, the adaptations that have served the cats so well in the natural world can work to their disadvantage in a world changed by man. The lion's prowess at killing large hoofed animals makes it difficult to raise cattle with lions lurking in the vicinity, so the cats have been persecuted by farmers in many parts of their range. The savagery with which a mother tiger defends her cubs makes it less likely that she and her offspring will be tolerated when the area in which they live becomes a center of human population.

Throughout much of the world, cats and people are increasingly coming into conflict. This is especially true in the developing countries of the Third World, the home of such species as the lion, tiger, leopard, and jaguar. Human populations are increasing, occupying land that once was wilderness. The demand for food, and for land on which to grow it, naturally is increasing as well. Jungles are being cleared, and people are putting the plow to the savannah.

Runaway human population growth is the greatest single threat to the wild cats, as it is to most other wildlife in the world today. It is what ultimately lies behind the deforestation, pollution, and general disturbance of the environment that, if allowed to continue, will destroy most of the wild world. The problem is most severe in some of the places where the grandest cats have their strongholds—not even the deepest jungles or the highest mountains are immune.

It is very easy for the resident of a comfortable apartment in New York City or Los Angeles to call for the preservation of forests and tigers in India, or of open plains and the lions that live on them in East Africa. But to understand the real problems of wildlife conservation today, it is necessary to assess the situation from the point of view of the people who are directly affected by wild animals. These people include the Indian woodcutter whose livelihood—and perhaps survival—may be threatened by the presence of large numbers of tigers in the forests where he works. They include the African farmer who needs land on which

to plant the crops that feed his family more than he needs the game herds and lions that live there.

Many developing nations, to their great credit, have undertaken truly meaningful programs to protect animals such as the endangered wild cats. These programs need support from the citizens of more prosperous lands—the type of support that has been provided by organizations such as the World Wildlife Fund and the New York Zoological Society. Without such groups, there would be even fewer of the wild cats roaming the earth than there are.

In the pages that follow, some of the basic facts that are known about the wild cats are set forth, and the animals are pictured as they go about their activities—hunting, feeding, mating, rearing their young, defending their territories, and just lazing about. In all these activities, the cats proclaim their status as sone of the most majestic of all wild animals. The wild cats are creatures to be admired and appreciated, not only for the important role they play as predators in keeping the world's ecology in balance, but for their own intrinsic qualities. These animals, at once fierce and gentle, stark and soft, frightening and beautiful, embody nature in its many aspects. If the cats were to vanish from the wild, perhaps the day-to-day lives of most people would not change significantly, but the world would be sadly impoverished by the loss.

13

1

CHAS. R. KNIGHT
1903

The Wild Cats: Their Origins

the landscape of western North America, where South Dakota, Wyoming, and Nebraska meet in a welter of badlands and prairies, has been sculpted by wind and water with brutal but breathtaking severity. In many places the earth has been scooped into great basins, dotted with the mounds of prairie-dog burrows, and rimmed by sheer, eroded cliffs. Interspersed among these immense bowls are areas where the terrain looks almost lunar. Like colossal beasts rising from the sea, barren buttes and bluffs rear jagged heads skyward, above a seemingly endless maze of canyons.

Stretching to far horizons, the stark panorama strikes many people as primeval. The truth is, however, that often in ages past the land was not nearly so rugged, and in fact looked downright gentle. This was the case during most of the period that scientists call the Oligocene epoch, between 35 million and 25 million years ago. Then, the region was one of grasslands that at their roughest were only slightly rolling. These broad plains were made lush by the periodic flooding of shallow rivers that meandered across the countryside.

In this peaceful Oligocene setting, a savage battle was joined one long-ago day by two fierce big cats. Scientists envision it because they have found the skull of one of the combatants bearing a wound believed to have been inflicted by the other. The wound is a hole punctured in the left frontal portion of the fossilized skull, evidently made by a large, saberlike canine tooth. This weapon was possessed by several big cats of the time, including the owner of the skull, a beast scientists call *Nimravus*.

Whether *Nimravus* tangled with one of its own kind or another sort of beast, no one can say for sure. The opponent may well have been another kind of large feline, because although the Age of Mammals was nowhere near its peak, several different kinds of big cats already had evolved to prowl the landscape. It seemed almost as if nature were experimenting with multiple versions of the basic feline model, testing their adaptability.

Primarily on the basis of teeth, the most abundant fossils, scientists have divided the early big cats into three basic groups. One was of animals with rangy bodies built for speed, and extra-long canines. *Nimravus* typified this class, known as the "false saber-tooths." Another group comprised robust animals with really huge upper canines, collectively called the "true" saber-tooths. The third consisted of big cats with what experts judge was "normal" dentition, bearing a resemblance to that of cats today.

For many years, scientists have held that modern cats were an offshoot of the false saber-tooths, perhaps even of something like *Nimravus*. The true sa-

Preceding pages: A true saber-tooth cat, re-created in this painting by Charles Knight, prowls the prehistoric landscape. Among the most awesome carnivores ever to live, the true saber-tooths probably preyed on large animals, including mammoths. Left: An old sporting drawing of a tiger.

ber-tooth cats were considered a bizarre evolutionary experiment that failed. Quite recently, this assumption has been challenged. On the basis of remains other than teeth, some scientists suggest that the true saber-tooths and the "normal" cats were closely related. The group characterized by *Nimravus*, they say, was an independent branch of the family tree that sprouted extremely early, then withered away after a while. According to this way of thinking, *Nimravus* has been improperly hailed as a prototype of modern cats. Instead, it was a very tentative attempt at making a feline, so primitive it hardly rates as one.

Scientists who study the evolution of animals have only begun to clarify the origins of the feline family, so there

remains considerable uncertainty about the lines through which it evolved. The cats are one of seven living families belonging to the order of mammals known as carnivores. The others are dogs, bears, raccoons and their relatives, weasels and theirs, hyenas and aardwolves, and a group known as the viverrids that includes civets, the mongooses, and the odd fossa of Madagascar, which so closely resembles a cat that scientists once classified it as one.

The first carnivores, from which all living families descended, appeared about 10 million years after the last dinosaurs perished. Small and weasellike, they were distinguished from the other primitive meat-eaters by several traits, one of the more evident being a large pre-

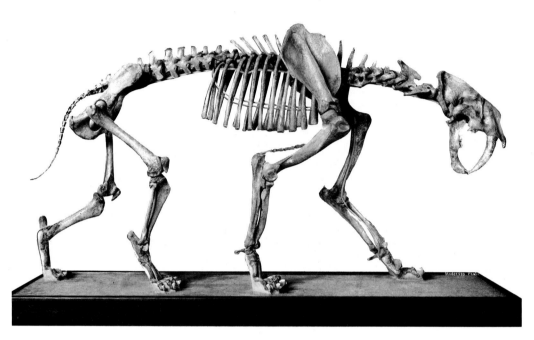

molar tooth in the upper jaw, and a molar in the lower, designed to cut and shear flesh. These teeth, known as the carnassials, remain a carnivore characteristic. The more primitive flesh-eaters—the opossum, for example—have largely undifferentiated teeth.

Through evolutionary paths discerned only darkly, the characteristics of the feline family gradually appeared in some of the animals descended from the carnivore root stock. Although there are plenty of obvious differences among the three dozen species of living cats, they share several important qualities, physiological as well as behavioral. Whatever their size, all cats have a form that is deep-chested and muscular, yet supple. The head is rounded, with a short muzzle. With one exception, the sexes look alike. The exception, a grand one, is the

lion. The famed leonine mane is sported only by the male.

A cat's eyes are set wide apart, giving it a broad field of view, a distinct advantage for a hunting beast. The pupil of the eye expands and contracts quite rapidly in response to changes in light level, which is why a cat quickly adjusts to seeing in the dark.

While not exclusively nocturnal, cats are generally active after sunset. Like many other creatures that often are abroad in the dark, the cat has a special reflector in its eye that helps it get the most use out of whatever light is available.

By way of explanation, consider briefly how the human eye operates. Images are formed when light is absorbed by the retina, which lies behind the eyeball and works like film in a camera. A certain amount of light, however, always passes

Opposite: Skeleton of the saber-tooth *Smilodon bonaerensis.* This cat was an American form. Left: Mortar in the shape of a jaguar from the Chavín culture of South America. For many pre-Columbian peoples, the powerful spotted cat represented divinity.

through the retina and is lost before it can be absorbed. In the eye of animals such as the cat, the escaping light is reflected by a mirrorlike layer of cells, called the tapetum, backing the retina. The light then bounces back to the retina, where it can be used. The chatoyance, or eyeshine, of a cat shown by the beam of a lamp at night is really the reflection from the tapetum.

Cats also have other aids to getting around in the dark. Sensitive whiskers help them feel their way. Their hearing is superb and is at least as important as vision in helping them to locate their prey.

Although each species has its own embellishments, cats share a basic hunting style. The hunter maneuvers into range by a rapid creep, punctuated by sudden stops, during which the body is so still it appears frozen. When the target is close enough, the cat launches its final rush—a matter of yards for the tiger, perhaps the better part of a mile for the hard-sprinting cheetah.

Whether sprinting, walking, or creeping, a cat travels on its padded toes, not flatfooted like a raccoon, bear, or, for that matter, a human. The rear feet of cats have four toes each; the front ones five. All but the fifth front toe, which is small, make contact with the ground when the animal is traveling.

Curving from the toes of cats are sharp claws, which, in all species but the cheetah, are retracted into sheaths when not in use. The claws help the cat to grab its prey. So do the canine teeth, particularly the upper ones, with which the big cats can deliver fatal bites to very large animals. The rest of the cat's twenty-

19

Top: Illustration of a tiger, from *A General History of Quadrupeds*, an 1834 book by Alexander Anderson. Bottom: Painting of a cougar by John James Audubon. This is taken from Audubon's classic book, *The Viviparous Quadrupeds of North America*, published in 1845.

eight or thirty teeth are used for chewing and scraping meat from bone. The latter task is also performed by the cat's sandpapery tongue.

The creatures that developed into cats may have arisen directly out of the viverrids, or from an animal that was the ancestor of both the cat and civet clans. However the cats evolved, the traits that characterize them were being put together in animals that lived at least 25 million years ago, and probably existed much earlier.

Hints of what the early cats may have been like can be perceived, with a little imagination, in a few types still living. One of these is the clouded leopard, an agile hunter of the tropical forests of Southeast Asia. Its skull is more elongated than the rounded heads of most other modern cats, as was true of earlier felines. Moreover, no other living cat has such large canines for its size. These daggerlike teeth are nearly as long in relation to its skull as were those of the ancient saber-tooths. Indeed, purely on the basis of its canines, the clouded leopard can be thought of as a modern-day saber-tooth. With its long canines, the clouded leopard can grab monkeys and birds while in the trees. The same cat, weighing only about 35 to 50 pounds, can kill creatures as large and rugged as wild boar and young water buffalo.

Another cat that may hold some very solid clues to the past is the strange little feline of Iriomote Island, in Japan's Ryukyu chain. The Iriomote cat (*Mayailurus iriomotensis*) was discovered only in 1965 and is exceedingly rare. Fewer than two score of the cats, so far as is known, roam the semitropical forest that clothes the island's interior. Since its discovery, the Iriomote cat has stirred debate. Some zoologists say it is no more than an isolated but close relative of the small leopard cat (*Felis bengalensis*), which is widespread in southern Asia. Others say it is unique, similar to the primitive ancestors of today's felines. They have some compelling reasons for thinking so. The Iriomote cat seems to share some traits with the viverrids, including external anal scent glands. Presumably, such scent glands may have existed in the earliest cats, or in their immediate predecessors, and then gradually disappeared through evolutionary changes.

Upholders of the Iriomote cat's primitive status also say it is similar in some respects to an important fossil cat, *Pseudaelurus*. Although *Pseudaelurus* was larger than the Iriomote cat, the two seem to have a similar bone structure. *Pseudaelurus* is yet another of those cats whose place on the feline family tree has been widely debated. It has been assigned myriad positions, from that of an aberrant oddball to the grandsire of the whole modern lot.

The most recent view of *Pseudaelurus* is that it is an early representative

of the line that produced the modern cats—the earliest found so far, in fact, dating back at least 25 million years. Several types of *Pseudaelurus* inhabited both the Old and New Worlds, and all were definitely members of the ancestral house of today's cats.

Out of this house, quite early, came the true saber-tooths. The cheetah (*Acinonyx jubatus*) branched off early, too. The main line led to felines ranging in size from the cougar (*Felis concolor*) down. The cats of *Panthera* constitute a major offshoot, sprouting perhaps from creatures much like the clouded leopard or snow leopard. They seem to have characteristics of both the *Panthera* cats and the cougar, or *Felis*, group.

Most of what is known about *Pseudaelurus* comes from fossil teeth and skulls, but a few other remains have been found, too. Together, the fossils have helped scientists reconstruct something of how this prehistoric cat looked and lived. *Pseudaelurus* was about the same size as a clouded leopard, but with longer legs. The length of its limbs is probably an indication that it hunted primarily on the ground, although there is no reason to believe that it did not climb trees as well.

As is the case now, the physique of prehistoric cats had a lot to do with how they hunted. Long-limbed *Nimravus*, for example, must have raced after its victims on the open plains. In all likelihood, it preyed mainly on herbivores of modest size. The same seems true of another lightly built false saber-tooth known as *Dinictis*, an early contemporary of *Nimravus*.

Contrasting with such sleek speedsters were massive-bodied cats that almost certainly hunted game that was big and slow. Apparently they relied on creeping close, rushing the prey from short range, and overpowering it in a short but violent battle.

Typical of the earliest cats of this sort was one called *Eusmilus*, a bulky false saber-tooth that some researchers believe may have punched the hole in the *Nimravus* skull mentioned earlier. *Eusmilus* stands out because it was lantern-jawed—its lower jaw protruded far downward and outward, like a heavy flange. This odd adaptation served a highly practical purpose. Covered by the cheek, it sheathed the cat's huge upper canines when the jaws were shut.

The true saber-tooth cats lacked the jaw flange of *Eusmilus*. They went about with sabers jutting far below their chins, giving them a monstrous look. The sight of one of these hulking creatures stalking across the countryside must have been terrifying. Almost certainly it was witnessed by human eyes, because the last and greatest of the saber-tooths lived within the time span of man.

On the scene when the first humans appeared, the true saber-tooths sur-

The tiger epitomizes the grace and power of the feline tribe. Among its many geographical races is the Siberian tiger, shown here, which is the largest living cat. The "typical" race is the Bengal tiger of the Indian subcontinent.

23

A picture of combined laziness and elegance, a lioness yawns in the sun of an African afternoon. Though lions are still abundant in some parts of Africa, they have disappeared from many other regions. Vast stretches of African savannah have been converted to farmland, destroying the habitat of the lion and its prey.

24

vived long after the arrival of our own species. The time was the Pleistocene epoch, when great ice ages repeatedly gripped the earth, with long warm periods between big freezes.

Pleistocene saber-tooths were barrel-chested, with massive shoulders, a huge neck, and a back sloping toward the rear. Their front legs were long and muscular, the rear ones short and rather slight. Their insignificant hindquarters, which terminated in a bobtail, made them appear to be all head and foreparts. Some of them seem so unevenly proportioned they appear almost awkward, leading to speculation that they were not fierce predators, but skulking scavengers that fed on the carcasses of other large animals. The prevailing opinion, however, is that they were hunters, not swift and agile, perhaps, but immensely powerful. Their herculean shoulders, chest, and front limbs were strong enough to hold down animals larger than they, as their sabers repeatedly stabbed into a vital spot.

To bring its sabers into play most effectively, the cat opened its jaws in a horrid gape, so wide they were separated by more than a right angle. This was made possible by a special hinge that allowed the lower jaw to drop so far it almost pointed rearward. The arrangement sacrificed strength for mobility, but no matter. The saber-tooth did not need to close its bite with great power, just to drive its monstrous canines deep into the flesh of its victim.

The prey of the saber-tooth cats seem to have been some of the largest mammals ever to walk the land. Bones found in what appears to have been the den of one saber-tooth, *Homotherium*, suggest it preyed on young mammoths. How the cat was able to do this without bringing the rest of the herd down on it is one of the secrets of the past.

Most of the saber-tooths vanished before the last of the ice ages. One, however, persisted until the end of glacial times. As recently as eleven thousand years ago, it roved the gentle valley in the shadow of the Santa Monica Mountains, where the city of Los Angeles sprawls today. This cat is *Smilodon*, the classic saber-tooth, a stump-tailed brute that swarmed about the famed La Brea Tar Pits—once a waterhole for Pleistocene game, now a magnificent source of fossils and the center of Los Angeles' Hancock Park.

Evidence that *Smilodon* thrived in the area has been left in the form of fossils taken from the tar pits, really beds of asphalt that even today underlie quiet pools of water in the park. The bones of more than 2,400 individuals of the savage cat have been found in the pits. *Smilodon* must have prowled the edges of the pools, drawn by the struggling animals that stopped to drink and became mired in the sticky, black goo.

One can imagine the cat creeping

Lions inhabited Europe as well as Africa and Asia well into historical times. Lion hunts were depicted in the art of pre-Homeric Greece more than twelve hundred years ago. The lion is so closely related to the tiger that hybrids of the two species have been bred in captivity.

up to the water's margin, watching the frantic attempts of a trapped victim. It might be a giant ground sloth, a Pleistocene bison, even a mammoth or mastodon; all probably were meat for *Smilodon*. Driven by hunger, *Smilodon* springs out over the asphalt to the broad back of the victim. Sinking in its claws, the cat thrusts its canines, more than half a foot long, into the prey. With its teeth embedded, the reason that *Smilodon's* nostrils were set far to the rear, almost atop its snout, becomes evident. The position permitted easy breathing while the sabers were jamming into the prey.

Frightful though *Smilodon* may have been, it was not the most terrible cat to hunt the region around La Brea. There was another, even bigger and more awesome, and without question the ruler of the countryside. Portending the future, it was not a primitive variety, but a feline of modern type, indeed, a member of the group *Panthera*.

Although the external appearance of the creature is still not certain, its full skeleton has been recovered. A fourth again as large as the biggest living tiger, it may have been either a colossal lion, as indicated by certain features of the skull, or an enormous jaguar. In the absence of anything more specific, it has been given a name that is most fitting, the "great cat," *Panthera atrox*.

The great cat combined a massive body with well-proportioned legs, and formidable jaws that, although lacking the mighty sabers of its contemporary, possessed tremendous strength and biting power. Its kingdom was the open savannah, where it must have been the terror of game herds.

Panthera atrox roamed almost all of North America at one time or another during the Pleistocene. Close relatives of equally impressive size inhabited the Old World. Among them was the huge cave lion, much larger than the lion of today but presumably the same species. Prehistoric artists painted its imposing portrait on the walls of European caves. They pictured the mighty lion as maneless, as some lions still are, sometimes with a touch of striping.

The rise of cats such as the great cat and cave lion trumpets the dominance of modern felines. By the ice ages they had spread around the world and were developing into the animals we know today. Even before the time of the glaciers, some cats remarkably like those of the present had evolved. More than two million years ago, there were lynxes and cougars that were little different from those in existence now.

Given the confusion over the origins of the modern cats, it is not surprising that zoologists have not sorted out all of their differences over kinship among the living species. Scientists do not all agree about which species should be grouped as close relatives and which

should be classified in different genera. As a result there is considerable variation in the scientific nomenclature of cats.

Be that as it may, cats of one type or another are native to most of the world, except for Australia and its environs, Antarctica, the West Indies, Madagascar, and some other islands. Domestic cats (*Felis catus*), however, have been introduced on several islands—those of the West Indies, for example—and after running wild have played havoc with native birds and other small animals.

The domestic cat's ability to live on its own reflects its close ties with its ancestors, believed to be the African wildcat (*Felis libyca*) and possibly the European wildcat (*Felis silvestris*). These belong to a large group consisting mostly of small cats, very similar to the domestic type, but also including a few large ones, such as the cougar. The cougar is matched or exceeded in size by several other cats, including the lion and tiger.

With a great variety of opinion existing as to the relationships among felines, it may be understandable that there is also a lack of uniformity about which species qualify as "big cats." Only four species have gained universal acceptance as big cats. Closely related, they all belong to the same genus, *Panthera*. In order of size, the group consists of the tiger (*Panthera tigris*), the lion (*Panthera leo*), the jaguar (*Panthera onca*), and the leopard (*Panthera pardus*).

Largest of all living cats, the tiger may weigh up to 600 pounds and reach a length of 13 feet from the tip of the nose to the end of the tail. Maximum size for a lion is a few inches shorter and a couple of pounds lighter. The weight limit of a jaguar, which grows to a maximum of nine feet long, is somewhere around 350 pounds. The leopard is approximately the same length as the jaguar, but it is more lithe. At the heaviest, it weighs just over 200 pounds.

Maximum size for a species, however, is attained by very few of its members—so few, in fact, that they are oddities. Even at 450 pounds, a tiger or lion is considered a real bruiser. So is a 200-pound jaguar. As a rule, the run-of-the-mill beast is much smaller than the biggest of its kind. Not surprisingly, therefore, most leopards are much lighter than 200 pounds, and many, especially females, do not even weigh half that.

Many leopards and even some jaguars, in fact, are smaller than individuals of species not always grouped with the big cats. What this adds up to is that size alone is not enough to gain a species across-the-board acceptance by the authorities as a big cat. There are scientists, for instance, who assert the title should go only to cats capable of roaring. These are the big four of *Panthera*. The ability to roar has nothing to do with size, however, but with the flexibility of the voice box. The cats that roar have voice boxes

A cheetah snarls a warning at an interloper. Although it looks fierce, the cheetah is remarkably docile for a large cat and is easily tamed. For centuries cheetahs were used as hunting animals by the nobles and kings of Asia. Kublai Khan was among the rulers who made use of hunting cheetahs.

that stretch more than those of other species, and thus produce a deep, throaty sound. The flexible voice boxes also allow them to bolt down chunks of meat the size of a football.

Because of what they view as similarities in bones or behavior, some experts group two nonroaring, smaller felines within *Panthera* and the big cats. These are the snow leopard, which seldom weighs more than 90 pounds, and the clouded leopard, hardly more than 40 or 50 pounds. Other scientists disagree, and classify each of the two independently, giving them the respective scientific names *Uncia uncia* and *Neofelis nebulosa*.

Obviously, within some very flexible limits the rating of cats as "big" can be fairly subjective. This book takes a broad view, gathering with the truly large cats some borderline species as far as size is concerned. Because of their fierce demeanor, great power, and natural nobility, they deserve a place among the grandest of felines.

Besides the roaring cats, this group consists of the snow leopard, the clouded leopard, the cougar, the cheetah, the three lynxes, and the ocelot. All are strong

29

Solitary and shy, leopards sometimes inhabit areas quite close to human population centers. The leopard is very arboreal, spending much time in the trees. Black leopards, such as the one shown here, sometimes occur, especially in Asia. They are merely a color phase of the normal variety.

enough to bring down prey as large as deer and antelope, and many take much bigger victims. All have such marvelous vitality and superb grace as to stir envy in the human breast.

Most of this book focuses on these larger cats, because they are the ones that are most spectacular. From an examination of their life style—the ways in which they stalk and kill prey, reproduce, rear young, and carry out all their other activities—a picture of the entire cat family can be gained. This is not to say that the smaller cats will be neglected. They too are covered in the pages to follow. While they may not be as awesome in purely physical terms, they are undeniably attractive, personifications of grace and often of beauty.

As the big cats spread and developed into distinct modern species, they adjusted to a remarkable range of environments, as contrasting as equatorial jungle and subarctic snows. People often associate big cats only with the tropics— dank, steamy rain forests and sun-baked plains in Africa, southern Asia, and South America. True, big cats of one type or another inhabit such places, but it is a misapprehension to believe that they all are best suited to regions at the earth's mid-section.

The tiger, for example, is as at home among the conifers of Manchuria as it is in the rain forests of Indochina or the swamps of India's Sundarbans in the Ganges delta. A look at where the tiger arose, and its original range, confirms

31

Jaguar populations, like those of almost all of the spotted cats, have been drastically reduced because of overexploitation by the fur trade. In much of its range, the jaguar is also threatened by ranchers because it sometimes kills livestock.

that—as for many big cats—a warm climate is not essential.

Tigers seem to have originated in Siberia, on the fringes of the Arctic, for their fossils have been discovered in the ice of islands in the region's north country. Before its range was diminished by human agency, tigers lived all across the Asian land mass, from the Siberian heartland to Bali, Java, and Sumatra. The original homeland of the tiger included such chill places as the bleak, craggy wilderness of eastern Turkey, a wild land dominated by Mount Ararat and pounded by blizzards in winter. Tiger country spanned the icy ravines of Szechwan in western China, stretching overland to the forbidding Tibetan plateau and the shores of the Sea of Okhotsk.

Unlike tigers, lions are children of the tropics, specifically of the boundless African savannah, where the whistling wind draws music out of the thorn bushes and the grasses grow lush in the rainy season. The lion, however, was not bound to the equator. In prehistoric times, with the Middle East as a bridgehead, lions moved east and west. They invaded Asia, reaching all the way to central India, and the heart of Europe, spreading as far west as the British Isles.

Since the end of the last ice age,

the lion's range has dwindled, at first because the open country was replaced by forest. Lions were frequently pictured on the friezes of ancient Assyria. The Greeks who were the subjects of the Homeric epics regularly hunted lions in the hills of their rugged homeland. The Persian king Darius the Great adorned his sumptuous palace at Persepolis with carvings of lions. Lions were relatively common in southern Europe as late as the time of the wars between the Greeks and Persians. The historian Herodotus, who lived in the mid-fourth century before Christian times, described lions as being very common in Thrace. When the Persian king Xerxes marched his army through the area in 480 B.C., lions attacked and killed some of his baggage camels. Only a century after Herodotus, Aristotle wrote that lions were rare in the same area where they had harassed the Persian army. By 100 A.D., the European lion was a memory—except in heraldry. Lions survived for many more centuries, however, in the lands on Europe's fringes. Mentioned 130 times in the Bible, the lion prospered in Israel until medieval times; the last one in that country was killed sometime in the thirteenth century.

Like the tiger and most other big cats, the lion has been victimized both directly and indirectly by people. Lions have been killed outright, often by poor farmers and herdsmen to protect themselves and their livestock. Even worse has been destruction of the environment in which the lion has evolved. Over ages of evolution, an animal adapts to living in certain surroundings. When these surroundings are suddenly altered, as happens when people upset ecological balances, the creature often cannot cope with the new situation and the species is imperiled as a result.

Gradually, over the centuries, lions disappeared from the Middle East, although as late as 1876, a British naturalist wrote that a valley near Shiraz, Iran, was "notorious for the number of lions found in its vicinity." The last of these lions was killed in 1923, and none has been seen in the largely denuded Iranian countryside since 1942. A few Asian lions survive in India.

The leopard had an immense range in historic times, and in the Pleistocene occupied an even wider territory. Then, it inhabited the entire Eurasian continent, and Africa from north to south. Since the ice ages, however, it has retreated from all but the southeastern fringe of Europe, the rugged mountains of the Caucasus in the Soviet Union. As proof that the leopard tolerates even extremely cold climates, its historic range has included parts of Siberia. At the same time, it does just as well in steaming jungle heat.

Also owner of a spotted coat, the cheetah, like the leopard, is native to both Asia and Africa. Most Asian cheetahs

A rover of Asia's high places, the snow leopard inhabits scattered mountain ranges from the Himalayas north to the fringes of Siberia. Few people have ever seen this cat in its native habitat, which is largely on rocky slopes well above the timber line.

Though it once ranged over most of North America, the cougar has now vanished from many places. In a few areas, the cat seems to be recovering, if only slightly. The cougar population of the eastern United States, for example, was believed extinct until zoologists discovered that a few cougars still roam the Appalachians.

have vanished, but a few remain in backwaters.

The original ranges of the snow leopard and clouded leopard were more restricted, and exclusively Asian. The snow leopard hails from the mountains of central Asia, while the clouded leopard is a jungle cat from the southern tier of the continent.

A band of three species, the lynxes are native to both the Old and New Worlds. The true lynx (*Lynx lynx*) is the only cat that in historic times has inhabited both. Sometimes reaching a weight of more than 50 pounds, the lynx originally ranged over the northern portion of North America and most of Europe, as well as northern Asia. Its range has diminished over the centuries. Britain lost its lynxes very early in historical times. So did Denmark. Elsewhere in Europe, the lynx persisted until quite recently, but since the last century it has suffered a sharp decline. Within the last hundred years or so, lynxes have disappeared from Switzerland, Austria, Italy, and most of Yugoslavia.

The smaller bobcat, or bay lynx (*Lynx rufus*), is solely an American animal, while the caracal, or desert lynx (*Lynx caracal*), is part of the fauna of Asia and Africa. Lynxes sometimes are classi-

fied as *Felis.* The ocelot *(Felis pardalis)* may weigh more than 30 pounds, the size of a large lynx, though it is usually much smaller. It lives from the middle of South America north to the border area of Texas and a small part of Arizona and New Mexico.

Also native to the Americas is the cougar (also called the puma or mountain lion). Once the most widely distributed land mammal in the Western Hemisphere, it lived from northern Canada to the tip of South America, from shore to shore on both continents. Years ago, however, it was driven from large portions of its original range, which included environments as different from one another as the high Andes and Rockies, South American jungle and North American spruce forest, desert, and wetlands such as the Everglades of Florida.

In prehistoric times, and for some centuries after, the largest American big cat, the jaguar, penetrated far into what is now the central United States, and as far east as Florida. Historically, however, it has been basically a creature of the tropics, where it reaches maximum size, although its range reached the state of California until about a hundred years ago, and southern Arizona until quite recently.

The heart of the jaguar's kingdom has been the middle of South America. From there, its range extends north to Mexico, and south to a little below Buenos Aires. Within this home the jaguar is sometimes found in a variety of surroundings, including forests, swamps, and parkland, but it fares best in thick jungle or heavy bush.

As the mightiest carnivore in its range, the jaguar inspired the awe of the humans who shared the land with it. To pre-Columbian peoples in South America, the big cat was symbolic of divine forces. Three thousand years ago, Indians living in the Peruvian highlands carved the grim faces of jaguars on the walls and pillars of their temples. From there, reverence for the jaguar fanned in all directions, especially north to Mexico. As centuries passed, many Indian peoples came to worship the jaguar as a savage and powerful god. Jaguar robes were worn by the high priests of the Mayan people, who created a dazzling civilization in the forests of Guatemala and Mexico's Yucatan peninsula. These Indians, learned in astronomy and mathematics, raised a towering temple to the jaguar god in the Guatemalan city of Tikal. The remains of the structure, which once loomed over the city's main square, still stand above the canopy of the jungle, which has been cleared around it. The cult of the jaguar god persisted after the Mayans had declined, lasting until the fall of the Aztec Empire in Mexico and the end of the native civilization there.

Whether or not representing divinity, the big cats have long been asso-

With its long, tasseled ears and expressive face, the caracal of Africa and Asia is one of the handsomest of cats. A southern species of lynx, it is a courageous, powerful fighter.

39

A silent prowler of North American forests, the bobcat is seldom seen and hardly ever heard, except during its breeding season. At that time, the bobcat can be unusually noisy, rending the night with its yowls and screams, which sound like those of a house cat but are a great deal louder.

ciated with power and vitality in the human mind. The leopard and lion show up frequently in the heraldry of medieval Europe. Tiger flesh still is eaten in China to improve health and sexual potency. The cheetah was trained as a hunter by eastern princes and potentates, and until recently was their favored pet.

While impressed by the big cats, however, people have not shied from persecuting them, sometimes for good reason, other times not. Literally since the dawn of history, man has waged war against the big cats, and the beasts have given ground—little by little at first, more recently with shocking suddenness.

Extensive and even organized assaults on the big cats are a product of more modern times, but overexploitation of the animals began long ago. The Romans, who drained the wildlife from much of the then-known world for shows in the arena, demanded a steady flow of lions for their bloody spectacles. Pliny tells of hundreds of lions used in single shows staged by Pompey and Caesar. Most of the cats they used were probably brought from northern Africa.

Overexploitation, systematic persecution, and environmental destruction drove lions, and later tigers, from many of their haunts, especially in the western world. Even so, they, along with the other big cats, continued to flourish for centuries in the extensive regions where people had not made an impact on the wilderness. Much of this sanctuary, at least in the Old World, was in the tropics.

About the time that Europeans began to "discover" the rest of the globe, the situation started changing. As the wilderness was breached, the havens of the big cats gradually disappeared. Yet the big cats remained abundant in much of the world until very recently. Even in the early years of the twentieth century, there were some forty thousand tigers in India alone. Today, only about four thousand of the world's largest cats survive in the wild.

Times are difficult, even dangerous, for the big cats. No longer are they the masters of their environment. Characteristics that aided their survival in nature over millions of years are not unfailingly effective in a world changed by man. Indeed, some of these traits actually work against survival. Extinction looms close to several of the big cats. None is so safe that its future is fully assured, although a few have made the best of a worsening situation.

The hope remains that things may get better for the big cats, if not everywhere, at least in enough places that their existence as wild creatures will continue. The world of the great cats has diminished but it has not yet disappeared. For now there is satisfaction in knowing that where the wilderness survives, and even in areas that are not so wild any more, big cats still walk the land. 41

The Wild Cats and Their Land

as the capital of Kenya, Nairobi is a thriving metropolitan complex with an urban core of broad avenues flanked by tall buildings and surrounded by suburbs, some quite posh by any standards. Into these suburbs, once darkness has descended, leopards occasionally wander, silently prowling the side streets, back yards, and gardens. Most of these nocturnal rambles go unseen by people; the only signs of them are pug marks—paw prints—found the next morning, or the absence of a family dog that has been taken as prey. Sometimes, however, people not only know about the visits, they come to expect them. One leopard, for example, nightly padded up the driveway of a large home and hauled itself atop the flat roof of the carport. Quietly, the beast would sit there, surveying the neighborhood, just as leopards do from the tops of kopjes, the small, rocky hills that dot the African savannah.

Leopards even venture past the suburbs, deeper into the city. One roving cat wandered into the industrial zone, entered a biscuit factory, and was trapped in a lavatory, creating a considerable ruckus when discovered by employees.

Nairobi is by no means the only city in Africa that plays host to leopards straying from the wild. Early in 1976, a leopard was shot by police in Pretoria, South Africa's capital, where sightings of the spotted cats are not at all rare.

Such incidents show how well leopards can adjust to the presence of large numbers of people, even near big cities. Their ability to do so reflects the creatures' overall adaptability to a multitude of different conditions, manmade as well as natural. All of the big cats have evolved traits that equip them superbly for survival in at least one type of natural environment, but few are as flexible as the leopard when it comes to coping with dense human populations.

Not only can the leopard get along near people, but it flourishes in almost every sort of environment that hosts any of the other big cats. Leopards live on the savannah—broad grasslands that remain dry for much of the year and grow green only during an annual rainy season. The savannah is a sea of grass, but it has islands of sparse woodland, often thorn trees, especially along watercourses. Scattered about the savannah, too, is thorn scrub. Even deserts, rocky with but a trace of rainfall each year, are the home of leopards. This applies to hot deserts such as those of Arabia, and cold ones, as in Iran and central Asia. Tropical rain forests—wet, seldom penetrated by sunlight, and with far fewer game animals than the plains—are also suitable for the adaptable leopard. So are temperate forests, of deciduous or evergreen trees, which feel the sweep of seasonal extremes from tropical heat to arctic cold.

As far as the environment goes,

44

Preceding pages: Despite their popular image as jungle cats, lions shun the deep forest. They are found on broad savannahs and sometimes in broken woodlands. Left: The leopard's spotted coat blends well with the patterns of light and shadow in dense foliage. Although at home in forests, leopards are not restricted to woodlands. They also inhabit deserts, plains, and mountains.

the requirements of the big cats range from uncomfortably specific to unusually catholic. Virtually across the board, the survival prospects of cats in the modern world parallel their environmental demands. The species that are least demanding are faring best. The leopard, with its marvelous versatility, is unquestionably the least imperiled of the four *Panthera* species.

Despite the sharply contrasting conditions under which different geographical groups of leopards live, there are no major differences among them, whether they live in Siberia, Java, Arabia, Zanzibar, the Congo, or any other place. Throughout their vast range—from the eastern margin of Europe, across Asia, and over the length and breadth of Africa—leopards have the same form and appearance. Yellow is the basic ground color of their coat, and it is covered with dark "spots," more properly called rosettes. Each of these markings is composed of smaller dark patches, arranged in a rough, ring-shaped pattern. Only on the face, tail, and limbs does a leopard have solid, relatively large spots. The body is long and lithe; only the neck and chest can be described as burly. The legs are rather 45

Leopards thrive in rugged terrain and frequently wander high into the mountains. They can be found well up on the mountains of eastern Africa, the Himalayas, and the Alburz range of Iran. The fact that the leopard can live at such heights indicates the cat's ability to tolerate cold weather.

short and terminate in paws that are so wide they appear oversize, which is why leopard tracks sometimes make the animals seem larger than they really are.

Virtually the only obvious differences among leopards from different places are in the length and shade of the coat, in the size of the spots, and sometimes in the animals' bulk. Leopards living in southern China, Indochina, and India have a red tinge to their coats. One West African race has a grayish shade to its pelt. The leopard that roams the high Alburz Mountains of northern Iran has exceedingly long fur. On the horn of Africa, leopards have short hair. Leopards in the Cape region of Africa have smaller spots than those in Uganda. The Sinai leopard is among the largest of its kind. Those of the Caucasus Mountains are rather small.

These are all minor distinctions and have little to do with the leopard's ability to survive in so many types of surroundings. More important is the cat's agility and immense strength, said to be the greatest, pound for pound, of any feline. Leopards regularly lug prey as large as moderate-size antelope into the branches of trees, where they can consume their food without being bothered by scavengers. They are marvelous jumpers, sometimes leaping 10 or 12 feet vertically to reach a perch or vantage point. Horizontal jumps of almost 25 feet are not uncommon.

As noted, leopards like to spend time on perches overlooking the landscape—trees in the forest, and rises or outcroppings in the open. Even when in an apparently exposed position, however, the leopard can be difficult to see. The spotted pattern of its coat, while it may seem to attract attention, is really a form of disruptive coloration that confuses the eye. The protective quality of the coat seems to work under any conditions, whether among the snow and rocks of high mountains, the jungle shadows, or the brown grasses of the plains.

Perhaps the greatest advantage the leopard has is its astonishing stealth. Leopards being trailed by hunters have a knack for disappearing when they seem about to walk into full view. This sort of behavior, which has been witnessed time and time again, casts the leopard in the role of a spotted wraith and has led many people to credit it with near-supernatural qualities.

There is nothing at all unnatural about how the leopard manages to be so covert. It is a quality made possible by numerous adaptations, ranging from superb eyesight, even in the dark, to the way the leopard walks, with the soles of its forepaws turned in, so that the outer border of the foot touches the ground before the full weight of the animal comes down. Even while walking two or three miles an hour—a normal pace—a leopard can halt in mid-stride the moment the margins of

its foot touch something strange or suspicious.

It is the secretive nature of leopards that enables them to live in a human environment, often without anyone being aware of their presence. This was the case for many years in Israel, where two still-surviving populations of the rare Sinai leopard existed for years before they were discovered.

The first group came to the attention of zoologists when pug marks were seen in the Judean wilderness, south of Jerusalem. Then, in 1974, scientists found a kill, the remains of an ibex that had been brought down by a leopard (or per-haps two, for when researchers kept watch a pair of spotted cats emerged from the night to feed on the dead wild goat). A search for more leopards was undertaken and eventually eight different animals were sighted.

A year or so later, another population was found a hundred miles from the first. This group, numbering at least three, was seen at the government nature reserve and tourist site at Ein-Gedi, on the Dead Sea, north of Jerusalem. An area of steep cliffs over which waterfalls drop into shimmering pools, Ein-Gedi was the site of a temple five thousand years ago and was inhabited from then until the

Preceding pages: The trees of broken woodlands that dot the East African savannah, especially along watercourses, are favorite resting spots of leopards. No other big cat within the leopard's range is such an adept climber. Left: The cougar inhabits a variety of environments, including wetlands and pine forests, but it seeks out mountains as a prime refuge throughout most of its range.

Middle Ages. It is said that King David came to bathe in the pools.

The Ein-Gedi leopards were first sighted by some Israeli soldiers, and the sighting was later verified by government game wardens. Since then the animals have appeared regularly. Tourists who have seen the leopards on the rocks have tumbled down embankments in their haste to get away from the cats, which have never made a menacing move. At least one of the leopards caused considerable upset in a nearby kibbutz, wandering the streets almost nightly and frightening passers-by.

Another, similar, case occurred in the Simian Escarpment region of Ethiopia, in 1974. A wildlife biologist who was visiting the area happened to be going down a road that cut through lands densely populated by farming families. A stone's throw from fields where farmers regularly worked, the tracks of a good-size male leopard were discovered. The animal was found to be living in a nearby gorge, emerging at night to feed on domestic livestock.

The availability of livestock as food actually has increased the numbers of leopards in some areas. There seem to be more leopards in the farming country near Gaborone, the capital of Botswana, 51

Though agile and powerful, the cougar is shy and usually tries to avoid people. Only a handful of seemingly unprovoked attacks by cougars on humans have ever been reported. Cougars are so secretive that people who have lived for years in cougar country seldom if ever see them, unless the cats are chased by hounds and treed.

than in the wild desert 60 miles away. Farmers in South-West Africa say that leopards now hunt in places where they did not live only a few decades ago.

None of this is to suggest that leopards abound throughout their immense range. On the contrary, while the limits of the range remain the same, leopards have vanished from most of it. Those that survive exist in pockets. Some of these are in national parks, although their most effective havens are determined not by political boundaries, but by environmental parameters. Rugged forests and, especially, mountains are the leopard's most secure sanctuaries.

The heavily forested interior of Sri Lanka, for instance, retains a sizable population of leopards. They still wander the mountains of South Africa's southern cape, from which the lion, the rhinoceros, and most other large animals have disappeared. In Kenya, the Aberdare Mountains rise to 12,000 feet from flat savannah that has been turned into a patchwork of farms and towns. Leopards, not often seen in the flatlands, are frequently encountered in the mountains.

How many leopards inhabit such places is hard to determine, because the cats' activities are so well hidden. One generally accepted estimate—and an estimate is all it is—places the number of leopards in all of eastern and southern Africa's parks and preserves at fewer than ten thousand. Several thousand more may

live outside the parks. A scientist who surveyed leopards in Ethiopia, for instance, estimated that up to three thousand may inhabit the southwestern part of the country, where the only sizable tracts of forest remain. Outside Africa, the figures are even more difficult to determine. Large numbers of leopards inhabit parts of southern Asia, but in the north the population has sharply decreased. Soviet scientists believe that there may be fewer than five hundred leopards left in all the U.S.S.R.

Among the most endangered groups of leopards are those of the Sinai, the interior of Iran and Iraq, and the desert country of Arabia and North Africa. Only a handful of leopards survive in Arabia; fewer than a hundred still hunt in the mountains north of the Sahara.

Like almost all other imperiled wild animals, the leopard suffers mainly from destruction of its habitat. Very few endangered or extinct animals owe their disappearance solely to other pressures. But other factors do play a part, and in the case of the leopard—and, indeed, the other big cats—a number of pressures have added to the drain on populations caused by habitat destruction.

Most of the big cats have been persecuted to some degree because, as predators, they compete with man for game and, more important, livestock. When people have firearms and poisons at their disposal, the competition tilts

52

Almost hidden in a lush wetland, this jaguar testifies to its species' fondness for water. Jaguars swim readily and often prey on aquatic animals such as caimans (relatives of the alligator) and large fishes. The capybara, a large water-loving rodent, is also a common prey of this big cat.

heavily against the cats. Most big cats—especially those with spotted or striped coats—also have been victimized by trade in their furs, legal as well as under-the-counter. The trade has now been severely restricted, but poaching remains a problem in many areas.

The leopard provides a vivid example of how a big-cat species can have many geographical races, similar but differing in slight details, and of what it takes for one of these large predators to survive in today's world. The cat that compares best with the leopard in the vastness of its range and in its capacity to live under markedly varied conditions is the cougar. This cat is so stealthy that game wardens have worked for years in the heart of cougar country without ever seeing it, although tracks and caterwauling continually indicate its presence.

Slender of body, with an unusually long tail that droops and then turns upward toward the tip, the cougar generally has a brown coat, although like the leopard it can be found in several shades, from gray to rusty. Extremely shy, the cougar spends most of the day under cover—in caves, among brush, or on hidden ledges. Most of the animal's wanderings are between dusk and dawn, although where cougars have not been subjected to harassment they sometimes are about before dark.

So graceful it seems to flow over barriers when it clears them, the cougar

54

has been known to make horizontal leaps of 30 feet and to sail over obstacles higher than a tall man's head. From a standing start, cougars have jumped a dozen feet up into the branches of trees or onto ledges. As for speed, the cougar is easily faster than the leopard and can run at more than 30 miles an hour over short distances. Exceptional vision, especially keen for movement, and good hearing also aid the cougar. However, its sense of smell, like that of all other cats, is not particularly well developed, certainly not nearly so much as in dogs.

Although their fur is not prized commercially, cougars have been the victims of intensive hunting, trapping, and poisoning throughout their range. The reason is that some of them—although by no means the majority—prey on livestock.

Like the leopard, the cougar still can be found over great areas of the earth, but with gaps between populations. Cougars have disappeared gradually, as wilderness has been opened up to logging, agriculture, and settlement. The cat has been driven north from the tip of South America but still remains in parts of Patagonia. In North America, where the decline has been most severe, the cougar was pushed back by the march of the frontier. Today it is common only from the Rocky Mountains west to the Pacific, but within that region it is abundant, even thriving in some places. All told, perhaps

In prehistoric times
jaguars ranged well
into the northern
regions of what is
now the United States.
Today, however, the
species is essentially
tropical. Only the
outer limits of its
range extend
marginally into the
temperate zones.

more than five thousand cougars inhabit this area.

One prime spot for cougars is Vancouver Island, British Columbia, site of the provincial capital, Victoria. About 60 miles wide and 280 miles long, the island remains heavily forested and is dramatically rugged, with deep valleys and a mountainous spine. It is one of the few places where cougars are seen with some regularity, even near heavily populated urban areas. At least one cougar has been shot in downtown Victoria, on the southern tip of the island.

The parallels between the life style of the leopard and the cougar are quite evident when it comes to living near urban areas and other places where the existence of such large predators is unsuspected by most people. Cougars still can be found within the city limits of Los Angeles and possibly, on rare occasions, not too far from New York City. They infrequently are reported in the mountains of New York and southern New England, even in the largely suburban state of Connecticut.

The Appalachian Mountains have proven to be the refuge for a race of cougar that until 1973 was classified as extinct by the United States Department of the Interior, despite reports of cougar sightings by woodsmen, sportsmen, and a number of scientists. Most zoologists and official conservation groups dismissed such reports as mistakes or wishful thinking. Eventually, sufficient evidence was accumulated so that the animals' existence could not be denied. The Interior Department issued a bulletin correcting its list of imperiled wildlife, changing the status of the eastern cougar from "extinct" to "endangered."

The best evidence in this sort of case is the finding of a dead specimen, which can be examined. While not helpful to the survival of the animals, it does provide solid proof of their existence. One of the events leading to the reclassification of the eastern cougar was the killing, in 1971, of a cougar in eastern Tennessee. The animal was identified as a truly wild creature, not a cougar of another geographical race that had escaped from captivity, as is sometimes true of animals that are seen where they are not supposed to be found.

It now appears that from a small, remnant population in New Brunswick, Canada, cougars have spread in small numbers through the Appalachians. No one knows how many survive, but scientists guess the total is only about two dozen. Some of the increase is due to the fact that farmland has been abandoned to woods, especially in the northeastern United States. At the same time, the cougar's main prey, the whitetail deer, has become considerably more common than it once was.

Whether the eastern cougar will become more abundant is impossible to

The forest that is the main habitat of the tiger has largely disappeared from southern Asia, especially in India. Habitat destruction is the major reason for the tiger's decline. Deforestation in Asia has been brought about primarily by exploding human populations and expanding needs for farmland and firewood.

predict, but given its remarkable adaptability, it should survive if given half a chance. Hopefully, the same is true of the only other cougar in the east, the so-called Florida panther, which once ranged across the southeast to the Mississippi. Between fifty and a hundred of these animals probably remain, mostly in Florida's backwoods and the Everglades. A few may also live in Louisiana and Alabama, where a small number of kills have been made in recent years. However, many zoologists believe that the dead animals were really escapees—from roadside zoos or misguided pet owners, for example—and not true wild members of the Florida group.

Unlike the cougar and the leopard, the jaguar has not adapted well to increased human presence. Except for rare strays, which may well be escaped animals, jaguars no longer are part of the fauna of the United States. South of the border they have declined considerably but still live in isolated country from Baja California to central Argentina, a little below Buenos Aires.

Big, feisty, and capable of destroying a man with ease, the jaguar has a reputation as a stock killer. While quite able to conceal its movements, the cat is not loath to defend itself when the need arises and is potentially much more dangerous to people than the cougar. For these reasons, it has been systematically destroyed

and driven out of agricultural areas and

cannot live side by side with large human populations.

Adult jaguars, with their considerable bulk, are not especially good climbers. They spend most of their time on the ground, although if pursued they will readily scramble into a tree if one is available. Their need for a warm climate, substantial cover, and a moderate supply of water limits the areas in which jaguars can live.

Like all big cats, the jaguar eats a variety of prey, from fish and frogs to large game animals. However, like the lion and tiger, it depends on sizable prey for sustenance. If such prey is entirely absent, the situation is untenable for the jaguar. The leopard, by contrast, can subsist entirely on small animals, and in fact can get by for a long time on a meal of one small fowl or rodent.

Leopards and jaguars, it is often said, look alike. However, when the lithe body of the leopard and the chunky frame of the jaguar are compared, it becomes evident that the resemblance is chiefly in the spotted coat. Even there, a signal difference can be seen. The jaguar has rosettes like the leopard, but most have a black spot in the center, separated from the outer ring by the animal's yellow ground color. Since the jaguar resides chiefly in brush, forest, and thickets, the coat is marvelous camouflage among the leaves and shadows.

Because jaguars inhabit deep for-

Expert swimmers, tigers enjoy the water and are seldom found far from it. One of the major habitats of the Bengal tiger, in fact, is the great mangrove swamp of the Sundarbans, in the Ganges delta. There tigers live amid a maze of seaside creeks and channels.

61

An inhabitant of both forests and bushy terrain, the ocelot is primarily a species of tropical America. It can sometimes be found as far north as the southwestern United States, but only in a few places very close to the Mexican border.

est and thick bush, and because they have a natural ability to stay out of sight, no one has been able to estimate how many of them exist, or even to study their habits very thoroughly. It is known, however, that great numbers of jaguars have been killed. Until the mid-1970s, when various national and international conservation agreements halted the commerce in rare cats, thousands of jaguar skins were shipped out of South America each year. In 1968 alone, almost fourteen thousand jaguar pelts were imported into the United States. This traffic has been virtually halted, but pressures on the jaguar continue.

The ocelot, like the jaguar, has been persecuted for its coat, which has dark spots on a gray to yellowish background. The ocelot's spots are solid, and some are so elongated that they resemble stripes. Although the ocelot can live in several different habitats as long as there is thick ground cover, it is mainly a forest animal like the jaguar.

Increasingly, the forest that supports the ocelot and the jaguar has been turned to ranch land. Because jaguars kill some domestic livestock, ranchers generally consider them vermin and wage war against them. A zoologist who went to one rather remote area of South America to study jaguars in 1978 had only begun his work when the cats he was trying to observe were shot by stockmen. The efforts of livestock interests, together with the elimination of the jaguar's habitat, have made the animal's future most uncertain.

The tiger, which numbers only a few thousand individuals in the wild, has much less rigid climatic needs than the

63

Unlike many wild animals, lions are easily propagated in captivity. Many zoos have lion prides that breed regularly, and some zoos have more lions than they know what to do with. Lions born in captivity can be released in the wild, but the wild habitats are quickly disappearing.

jaguar, but like it must have water, cover, and large prey. This last requirement is particularly important, because while a tiger even eats fruit when very hungry, it needs an average of 18 pounds of meat daily to keep up its strength and health. Hungry tigers have eaten twice that amount when they felt the need to gorge.

Adapted to most types of forest and grasslands broken by woods, the tiger is seldom found in wide-open country, another similarity with the jaguar. Its coat, which has an orange to red ground color marked by transverse black stripes, blends well into sun-dappled vegetation. Despite its size, a tiger can fade into even a scrap of woodland, almost like a Cheshire cat vanishing in the air. Occasionally, however, the fringe of white that runs from the chin along the underside of the body gives the animal away. If the tiger is approached from the rear, it sometimes is possible to spy the vivid white spot that stands out against the black fur on the back of each ear.

Packed with muscles that ripple forcefully when the animal walks, the tiger's forelimbs are extremely strong, equipping the animal well for killing large prey such as deer and even wild cattle. As a rule, the tiger is not particularly aggressive toward people, but rarely, like some of the other big cats, an individual tiger will turn into a man-eater.

For the most part, however, the tiger is content to seek its prey among its

64

The pride is essentially a society of lionesses. Male lions leave their native pride on reaching adulthood. They may then join another pride, but they are usually only temporary members. Females generally remain for life with the pride into which they are born.

Although adult lions usually do not climb trees, they have taken up this habit in a few parts of Africa, including the Masai Mara Game Preserve in Kenya. The reason for this unusual behavior is not known for certain. Some zoologists believe the lions go into the branches to escape biting flies.

fellow denizens of the wild. Unfortunately, though, the habitat needed to support game for the tiger has been ravaged over much of its range. The reasons are multiple, and they stem mainly from exploding human populations. Overgrazing by livestock, poor agricultural practices leading to erosion, and cutting down of shrubbery for firewood are just a few causes of habitat destruction. Finding normal prey gone, tigers turn to domestic stock—and reap a bitter reward.

At the same time, the tiger has been excessively exploited for the coat that provides it with such magnificent camouflage. Thousands upon thousands of tigers have been slaughtered so their hides could be turned into coats, rugs, and similar items. The tiger, moreover, is one of the few animals whose numbers have been seriously reduced by sport hunting. During the last century, especially in India, tigers were shot for sport without any thought of conservation. The perpetrators were primarily native Indian nobility and officials of the British raj. Some individuals shot as many as a thousand cats within a few years.

The result of these pressures was catastrophic. In 1930 it was estimated that in India alone there were forty thousand tigers, and probably as many throughout the rest of Asia. Today fewer than two thousand tigers survive on the subcontinent and its fringes, and perhaps four thousand worldwide. Several races

68

have vanished, and others are perilously close to extinction.

Within a single generation, the race of tigers inhabiting the beautiful island of Bali perished. So, very likely, has the Caspian tiger of northern Iran, Turkey, and Afghanistan, although a few may hold out in remote areas. The Javan tiger is down to about a dozen individuals. It is unusual in that its stripes sometimes break up into a spotted pattern, as they do on the Sumatran tiger, which numbers fewer than five hundred animals. The Chinese tiger is very rare, but its exact numbers are unknown. The massive Siberian tiger, with the least intense coloration and the thickest coat of any of the groups, is less common in the wild than in zoos, where hundreds have been bred. Only about two hundred wild Siberian tigers remain, scattered through the easternmost Soviet Union, northeastern China, and North Korea.

A slight increase may have occurred among the tigers in North Korea, at least in the demilitarized zone separating it from the south. War has sometimes helped the tiger by turning previously inhabited countryside into no man's land. It is believed that the Indochinese tiger, numbering about two thousand individuals, increased during the hostilities in Southeast Asia. The reason given is gruesome. The tigers apparently fed on battlefield casualities. Be that as it may, if any race of the tiger is to be saved, the Indo-

A group of cheetahs rests in the shadow of East Africa's Mount Kilimanjaro. In this area, cheetahs are a popular tourist attraction. A group like this often draws a swarm of cars and buses. Scientists worry that too much interference by tourists will be injurious to the cheetahs, which are becoming increasingly rare.

71

chinese is a likely candidate. Tigers of this group can be seen within 90 miles of large urban areas such as Bangkok, Thailand's capital.

International conservation organizations, chiefly the World Wildlife Fund, are making a desperate effort to halt the tiger's slide to extinction by helping India, Nepal, and other countries establish sanctuaries for the animals. A positive step has been the nearly global curb on the trade in tiger skins, although they still can be found in some markets in southern Asia. Until the mushrooming human populations of tiger country are controlled, however, the beast will be in deep peril.

Since both tigers and lions inhabited large portions of Asia in historical times, the question often is asked whether they ever shared the same territory. While it is impossible to say for certain, their differing environmental preferences probably kept them apart, even when their ranges were close or overlapping. The lion's life style is the opposite of the tiger's woodsy ways; as long as there is a choice it sticks to the open plains.

Lions make their living by their ability to hide in the tall savannah grasses or among the low thorn scrub. Two or three lions can disappear in the shadows of even a small thorn bush, a yard or so high. They can be invisible from only a dozen feet away. Their tawny coats aid concealment, especially when the grass is brown, which it is most of the time.

Like the other cats of great size, the lion needs lots of meat, even more than the tiger, and depends almost exclusively on the great herds of game that flourish on the plains. Though they are strong enough to make prodigious 25-foot leaps, lions generally do not engage in this sort of activity. They really are not built for running and leaping or, for that matter, climbing. Occasionally, however, they do make their way aloft into the large acacia trees that grow in clumps on the savannah. In two East African preserves, Lake Manyara National Park of Tanzania and the Masai Mara reserve in Kenya, lions habitually laze in the trees. Several of the cats can be seen at one time, sprawled in the green boughs. Why they do it is something of a mystery, although it may be to escape the biting flies that hover near the ground.

According to some estimates, there are 200,000 lions in Africa. Despite its numbers, there is no guarantee that the lion will continue to prosper. The savannah on which it depends is increasingly being converted to farmland; in many places farms cover the landscape as far as the eye can see. Large game herds have become a thing of the past, except perhaps in national parks, which themselves are often ringed with homesteads. Lions regularly turn stock killers—and suffer for it.

Already, in the last century, two

Although the cheetah likes open landscapes, it will retreat into broken woodlands on the savannah if human activities cause too great a disturbance. Of all the big cats, the timid cheetah is the least adaptable to changing conditions.

73

The long legs of the cheetah proclaim that it is a hunter that sprints after its prey in open country. This easily tamed cat, used for centuries by Asian nobility to course game, is now near extinction in Asia.

gorgeous races of lion have vanished, at opposite ends of the African continent. The largest lion of all, that of South Africa's Cape, was exterminated a hundred years ago. The Cape lion was known for its very large size and luxuriant black mane. It was wiped out so quickly after southern Africa was settled by the Boers that very little is known about its total range or about any peculiar habits it may have had. The Barbary lion of North Africa last prowled the landscape shortly before the Second World War. Its demise was due largely to the destruction of the mountain forests that supported the Barbary stag and the other hoofed animals on which it preyed. Some conservationists suggest that the way to ensure that lions survive outside parks—on ranches, for ex-

ample—is to provide an economic incentive for keeping them, such as regulated trophy hunting. Otherwise, the lion's numbers will dwindle to practically nothing within a few decades.

The last of Asia's lions live a pitiful existence, depending for food on goats and handouts from the wardens in northwestern India's Gir Forest. Covering 500 square miles, the forest is located on hills that rise to more than 2,000 feet above the adjacent lowlands. Some of the area is true forest, with towering teak trees, but most of it is open scrubland, tolerable for lions, if not the best of all habitats. Besides, there is nowhere else for them to go, because the area around it has a population density of nine hundred people per square mile.

Nominally, the Gir Forest is a preserve, but that is not really the case. More than five thousand native herders and seventeen thousand cattle inhabit the sanctuary. Valley floors are almost all cultivated, and logging goes on apace. During the summer, when the monsoon brings two feet of rain to an otherwise arid region, the Gir is visited by thousands more cattle as other herders drive their animals into it. Most of the area outside the forest is badly overgrazed, and now the forest itself is literally being eaten up as well.

Stripped and trampled, the forest is dying, destroyed by cattle. The lions clinging to existence there—fewer than two hundred—have little in the way of prey except for the herders' cattle and water buffalo, plus animals staked out for them by park wardens. The lions not only kill the livestock, but feed on carrion, unless the region's poor "untouchables" find it first. These people eat the meat of the dead cattle and sell the hides, going so far as to drive lions away from their kills to get the carcasses.

The situation is desperate, because it appears that the Gir is finished as a habitat for wildlife and soon will be useless for livestock as well. A few of the Gir lions have been moved to other reserves, and this technique offers a slim chance for saving them in a semiwild state. For lions to disappear from the Indian countryside would be especially ironic, for it is the lion, not the tiger, that appears on

This is one of the few photographs ever taken of a snow leopard in its natural habitat. It was taken in the Hindu Kush by George Schaller, a biologist with the New York Zoological Society. Schaller is one of the only scientists to have studied this big cat in the wild.

77

the country's ancient national crest.

A glance at the cheetah makes it obvious that this cat, like the lion, belongs to the wide-open countryside. More than any other cat—indeed, as much as any carnivore—it is built for sprinting. It has a deep chest that houses large lungs, a slim waist, and strong, very long legs, which can carry it to speeds of 70 miles an hour for several hundred yards.

Unlike any other cat, an adult cheetah cannot retract its claws. The claw sheaths that the cheetah is born with soon disappear, making it impossible for the animal to cover the claws when they are not in use. When the adult travels, therefore, the claws touch the ground, just like those of a dog. This fea-

Perhaps never very numerous, snow leopard populations have been reduced by excessive hunting for the fur trade. Responsible furriers no longer use the pelts of such rare cats, and several nations, notably Pakistan and the Soviet Union, actively protect the snow leopard. However, the animal is still hunted by poachers.

ture is assuredly no disadvantage for the cheetah, which hunts more like the members of the dog family than the other cats.

It is only on fairly level ground, in the open, that the sprinting abilities of the cheetah are really effective, and thus it never lives in forests. The cheetah has declined as a result of the same sort of environmental pressures as those affecting the lion, pressures arising from the agriculturization of the savannah. Moreover, with a yellow coat marked by attractive, solid black spots, the cheetah also has been exploited for its fur. The result is that only a few thousand remain, almost all in Africa.

Of all the big cats, the one that is the most specialized is the snow leopard, mysterious inhabitant of the high mountains of central Asia. Ranging from Afghanistan to western China, and from the border of Mongolia and the U.S.S.R. south to the Indian frontier, the snow leopard seldom descends to altitudes lower than 5,000 feet, and often lives much higher. During the summer, the animal often roves far above the timber line, on the crags and over the alpine tundra at almost 20,000 feet. At slightly lower altitudes, the Asian mountainsides are covered with dense thickets of rhododendrons, and here too the snow leopard wanders, hunting wild goats and sheep. When blizzards ravage the highest peaks, the game descends into the valleys, and the snow leopard follows, pushed not so much by the severity of the weather as by the movement of its prey.

The snow leopard is beautifully adapted to the harsh conditions of the high mountains. Its magnificent coat is long and thick, with a woolly underlining. So plush is its fur that the leopard seems much larger than it really is. The fur is pale gray, cream along the belly, and marked with very large rosettes, similar to those of the true leopard, but much bigger. In winter, the background gray lightens, but winter or summer, the animal blends well with the rocks and snow of its home. Marvelous insulation, the snow leopard's coat provides protection against the cold, and when necessary against the heat of the sun. Even the soles of the feet are furred, giving additional protection, and also making the paws natural snowshoes.

Another adaptation to living at dizzying heights is the snow leopard's ability to jump. How far it can leap is not really known, because few studies ever have been made of the snow leopard, except those by Dr. George Schaller of the New York Zoological Society. Its leaps are said to be awesome, and the cat is reputed to turn somersaults in midair. So grand is the animal's reputation for jumping that zoos fear to exhibit the snow leopard in moated or fenced enclosures, as is commonly done with lions and tigers.

No accurate count has ever been

Few people ever glimpse the gorgeous clouded leopard in its native home, the forests of Southeast Asia. Like the snow leopard, the clouded leopard is actually not a true leopard, but a totally different type of cat. Little is known of its habits.

made of the snow leopard population, because of its remote and scattered havens. However, scientists believe that in all of central Asia there are only a few hundred of what probably is the world's most beautiful cat. Despite the inaccessibility of its home, the snow leopard has felt the pressure of man. It has been killed for its coat, and even in the high mountains overgrazing and other forms of habitat destruction have diminished the wild sheep and goats on which the cat preys. While the snow leopard now is legally protected in most places, its future is no more certain than that of most other big cats.

Rivaling the snow leopard in the beauty of its coat is the smaller clouded leopard, which lives in the deepest forests of southern Asia and on islands adjacent to the mainland, including Borneo and Taiwan. The coat, gray to brown, is marked with dark stripes and blotches, which give it the "clouded" effect.

Like the snow leopard, the clouded species is a mysterious animal, and for the same kinds of reasons. It inhabits only the thickest jungle, and even there it is seldom seen, for it spends almost all of its time hidden in the leafy forest canopy. With a long tail that serves as a balancing aid, and very short legs, the clouded leopard is well suited to the trees. It even can travel upside-down along branches and hang by just one rear paw. It is not nearly

81

In North America, the bobcat (opposite) has a more southerly range and more varied habitats than the lynx, which sticks to boreal conifer forests. The European lynx (right) inhabits a number of different environments, including both hardwood and conifer forests.

Sometimes called the desert lynx, the caracal prowls mostly by night, hiding among boulders and brush during the day. Like the cheetah, it was once tamed by Asian nobility and used as a hunting beast.

as graceful on the ground, where the shortness of its legs is a considerable disadvantage.

So infrequently observed is the clouded leopard that, except for the group living on Taiwan, the status of the species is not at all certain. The Taiwanese race is in trouble, however, and it is likely that the deforestation occurring throughout much of the rest of the animal's range is very much to its detriment.

Just as the clouded leopard sticks to the forests of the tropics, the lynx is a creature of the forests in north temperate lands, up to the southern fringes of the Arctic. The animal remains common in North America, but in western Europe it has been pushed to the far north and a few last mountain refuges. In European Russia and Asia, lynxes seem to be doing well. One rare race of lynx, thought by some zoologists to be a separate species,

84

inhabits the Pyrenees and a few other wildernesses of the Iberian peninsula. Spots are not typical of all lynxes, and on some the gray-to-tan fur is hardly marked.

As a resident of northern lands or mountainous areas, the lynx lives for several months each year in deep snow. An obvious adaptation to this condition are its extra-large feet, cushioned with thick hair, which make even better snowshoes than the paws of the snow leopard. While the lynx has rather long legs, enabling it to move quickly for short distances on the ground, it is also a good climber and will ascend a tree to get out of danger.

Looking much like a smaller version of the lynx, with a slightly rustier coat, the bobcat has made the break with the deep forest, although it can live there as well as in almost any other habitat, except jungle and treeless plains. The bobcat, still relatively common in many areas, ranges from southern Canada well into Mexico. It is in every sense an all-around cat—an able climber, fast runner, and good swimmer. The bobcat is not found nearly as far north as the lynx, which is reflected by its paws, not as large or heavily furred as those of its bigger relative. Bobcats are among the big felines that regularly live amid large human populations—no other large cat is so often found in such surroundings. Not surprisingly, the bobcat is an extremely secretive animal, as much so as the cougar, and its presence usually is not detected except in breeding season, when it rends the darkness with yowls.

Its tasseled ears proclaiming its kinship with the lynxes—although not all scientists agree that the two are related—the caracal is built for swift movement, but not for running over long distances. Slim and long-limbed, it inhabits much the same sort of country as the cheetah, and originally the two cats shared a similar range. While still abundant in much of Africa, however, the caracal no longer is seen over the major portion of its Asian homeland, although it is not yet extinct there.

The caracal lives by quickness and agility. When in action, it moves like a brown blur. With so much of its habitat arid, the cat might seem hard-pressed to find water to drink, but it quenches its thirst easily with the body fluids of its prey.

Of all the adaptations that equip the big cats for life in their particular habitats, none are more striking than the behavioral and physiological characteristics that contribute to hunting success. These traits have evolved through natural selection over many millennia and have shaped the big cats for living most successfully in fairly well-defined environments. It is only when natural conditions have been drastically upset by human activities—a fact of life in today's world—that the big cats have difficulty in coping with the problems of survival.

85

3

Like the lynx, which stalks it through the coniferous forests of northern North America, the varying hare has huge, furry paws—the "snowshoes" from which its more familiar name, "snowshoe hare," derives. The function of these oversize feet is the same for both hare and cat: to provide traction on ice and support in snow. This parallel adaptation to a shared environment reflects a much deeper relationship between the lynx and the hare. Although the cat sometimes eats other animals, ranging from mice to deer, its existence depends ultimately on the hare, its chief prey throughout its New World range.

There is no more graphic example of the bonds between predator and prey than those of the lynx and the hare on which it feeds. In fact, the lynx population rises and plummets unfailingly in accordance with that of the hare. Records of the furs taken by the Hudson's Bay Company in Canada for almost two centuries clearly document this phenomenon. Once every decade, the hare population peaks, so that in some places the creatures literally cover the landscape. The following year, the number crashes, while the lynxes, having enjoyed a bountiful food supply the year before, multiply explosively. By the time another year passes, the cat population, now deprived of its prey, begins to diminish almost as rapidly as it increased. The hares, in turn,

start to proliferate again.

The survival of all big cats, of course, depends on that of their principal prey. Usually the prey is not so specific as a single animal, but consists of a group of similar creatures, such as various antelope or deer. Therefore, the correlation is not always so evident as in the case of the lynx and snowshoe hare.

Whatever the combination, hunter and hunted are entangled in a web of relationships that in turn are part of a broader ecological network. They have evolved together, each creature's adaptations mirroring those of the other as they exert a mutual influence on one another. One powerful interaction, for instance, is the defensive behavior of prey in response to the hunting tactics of cats.

Each big cat lives on a particular type of victim in given surroundings. Another way of expressing this is that the adaptations enabling a cat to survive in certain environments are largely, although not exclusively, devoted to hunting. The cheetah, for example, is adapted not only to running on flat, open savannah, where brush is sparse, but to running down small antelopes over that sort of grassland. The modification of the lynx's foot for travel in deep snow also enables it to overtake and kill other animals.

The lynx takes advantage of the snow to kill red foxes, which it pursues with what seems to be consuming vengeance. Though faster and more agile

Preceding pages: The world's fastest land mammal, the cheetah puts on a blinding burst of speed in pursuit of prey. It is able to accelerate to 70 miles an hour, but can maintain this speed for only a short distance. Left: A lion charges through the grass of the East African savannah. Male lions seldom hunt. Instead, they appropriate part of the prey killed by the lionesses.

than the lynx, the fox is at a disadvantage in deep snow—it sinks and becomes an easy target. Often lynxes seem to kill foxes out of sheer detestation, not touching them for food. In times of famine, however, the fox serves nicely as a meal.

When a lynx is famished and hares are scarce it will eat almost any animal it can kill. The victims may include large deer, caught while they are bogged down in snow or in a weakened condition. Most deer taken by lynxes, in fact, are old, sick, or outcasts from the herds.

As long as hares are plentiful, however, they are the lynx's mainstay. In-

stead of having to wander far afield in search of food, the lynx can confine its hunting to one or two square miles of territory. When there is an abundance of hares, the lynx often has only to wait motionless until one crosses its path. It then ambushes the prey. If the hare does not come to the lynx, the lynx stalks it, low and close to the ground. Once the hunter is within a few yards of the target, the preferred tactic is a rush or leap to kill the quarry. More often than might be suspected, the cat misses and must hunt again. One study in North America indicated that fewer than 20 percent of the

A lion stands quietly while a herd of wildebeest grazes peacefully not far away. Game animals seem able to sense when lions are hunting and when they are merely passing by. If the lions are not hunting, the animals usually do not bolt, though they keep a safe distance.

attacks by lynxes on hares are successful.

In Eurasia, the lynx is not nearly so dependent on the hare for its diet. The reindeer and even the red deer, a close cousin of the North American wapiti, are frequent victims. Lynxes sometimes even tackle wild boars, among the fiercest of creatures. Grouse and other ground nesters also furnish the Old World lynx with much of its sustenance. Rabbits and hares are by no means ignored, but it appears that only in a few places do they constitute even half of the cat's diet.

Among the regions in which lynxes take a heavy toll of rabbits and hares are two that are among the last remnants of primal wilderness in Europe. One is the Bialowieza forest, a hunting ground of medieval royalty, which lies on the border of Poland and the Byelorussian Soviet Socialist Republic. Now managed by state forestry authorities, the area has remained remarkably similar to the deep woods that covered central Europe more than a thousand years ago. Oaks grow to a diameter of seven feet at breast level, and spruces tower 170 feet. The woods teem with deer, wild boar, and game birds, all of which are eaten by the lynx, but hares are the predominant food.

The second wild region is the Coto de Doñana of southwestern Spain, near the delta of the Guadalquivir River. It is a basically flat area of sand dunes, pine woods, oak scrub, thickets of giant heath, and shallow marshes. Until re-

cently, rabbits were the chief prey of the lynxes here, but their importance in the lynxes' diet has declined because their numbers were drastically reduced by an epidemic of the viral disease myxomatosis. The cats have since turned more heavily to other game.

Lynxes inhabit other portions of the Iberian peninsula as well, among them mountainous regions such as the Sierra Morena of the south and the Pyrenees in the north. The Iberian, or pardel, lynx is thought by some authorities to represent a species distinct from the northern type. Not all agree with this classification, but there definitely are differences between the two. The pardel lynx is much more heavily spotted and, unlike the typical lynx, does not inhabit thick forests. Instead, it seems to prefer scrub, especially the mix of low oaks, evergreens, and dense thickets called *maquis* in Europe, similar to the chaparral of western North America.

The caracal also hunts in the scrub, but it prefers areas that are more open than the *maquis*, such as the savannah, a combination of scattered low thorn bush and grassland, sometimes verging on semidesert. Stalking and springing from close up, the caracal catches small antelopes, rodents, hyraxes, and ground birds. Even ostriches and eagles fall victim to the caracal if it finds them on the nest. Frequently the caracal uses another hunting tactic, one that requires dazzling

A lioness makes her final rush toward prey. A lion or lioness may stalk prey or wait in ambush, but always attacks with a powerful charge from a short distance. If the prey escapes, it is seldom chased more than fifty or a hundred yards.

93

Opposite: A lioness ends the life of a wildebeest with a bite in the throat. Even a large wildebeest is no match for a single lion or lioness.
Left: This lion is dragging its prey from the site of the kill to a quiet place, where the victim will be eaten.

speed and balance. Incredibly, it can hurl itself several feet off the ground to snatch small birds from the air. The cat is so swift that it can take several birds in one leap. Springing into the midst of a flock, the caracal can kill the better part of it before falling back to the ground. The birds are literally clawed out of space.

Both caracals and lynxes often hunt by night. The more secretive bobcat is almost exclusively a nocturnal hunter. Like the lynx and the caracal, it depends on stealth to get close to its prey. A New World species, the bobcat shares part of its range with the North American lynx, but its selection of prey more closely resembles that of the Old World lynxes. Whereas the American lynx sticks to one species of prey except in times of emer-

gency, the bobcat eats a wide variety of animals—small rodents, game birds, sometimes even reptiles. It is true that in most places rabbits and hares constitute about half the bobcat's diet, but even these are not limited to a single species.

Because the bobcat routinely preys on such a wide variety of animals, the decline of any one species does not affect it the way the varying hare's periodic population crashes affect the lynx. Moreover, the choice of prey gives the bobcat greater latitude when it comes to the type of country in which it can survive. The bobcat's great adaptability is due in large part to the diversity of its diet.

The same is true of the cougar, which also has a cosmopolitan diet. Deer are its choice, but it readily eats all sorts 95

After a hunt (right), a leopard consumes its prey in the branches of a tree (opposite). Leopards commonly haul their victims into the trees to eat. Above the ground, the leopard need not fear that lions or hyenas will try to appropriate its kill.

of other creatures, depending on availability. In the Rocky Mountains cougars have been seen killing mountain goats and bighorn sheep. The wild llamas known as guanacos are often the prey of cougars in southern South America. Mice, fish, and wild turkeys are all pleasing to the cougar's palate, as are other felines, including the lynx. Cougars regularly kill porcupines and beavers, which often constitute a substantial portion of their diet. An illustration of how avidly cougars sometimes seek out beavers occurred in the 1930s, on Vancouver Island, British Columbia. The beaver population of the northern part of the island was nearly wiped out by cougar predation.

While cougars easily exist on animals such as those mentioned above, they truly prosper where deer are abundant. Pudu and guemals—both small deer that live in the mountains—as well as a few other species are hunted by cougars in South America. In North America, cougars sometimes prey on wapiti and moose—generally aged, young, or ill individuals—but their chief victims by far are two other species: the whitetail in the east, the mule deer in the west.

The original range of the cougar in eastern North America coincided with the region in which the whitetail was

After stalking carefully to get within range (right), the cheetah bursts from concealment after its prey. Two of the fleet cats (opposite) join forces to chase a springbok over the stony plains of southern Africa. The springbok is one of several small antelopes on which cheetahs prey.

most plentiful. As noted in Chapter 2, the emergence of the eastern cougar from apparent extinction has come at a time when the whitetail deer is flourishing as it has not since the days of the pioneers.

A classic example of what happens when people disrupt the balance between prey and predator occurred early in this century, when cougars were eliminated from the Kaibab Plateau of Arizona. This area, more than a million acres situated 8,000 feet above sea level and bordered on the south by the immense gorges of the Grand Canyon, supported a large mule deer population. When sheepmen and ranchers arrived at the plateau in the

late nineteenth century, the herd numbered about three thousand. The chief predator was the cougar. A handful of wolves, plus coyotes and bobcats, also took a few of the mulies.

By the turn of the century, the herd had begun to diminish because of competition from grazing livestock and pressure from sport hunters. In an attempt to reverse the decline, President Theodore Roosevelt ordered—and personally participated in—a massive program of predator control. Nearly seven hundred

cougars were killed between 1906 and 1923. At the same time, all hunting of deer was halted by the United States Forest Service, which controlled the area.

Once killing of predators began, the deer seemed to prosper. The herd increased to an astounding 40,000 animals, then to 100,000 by the summer following the end of the control program. Foraging is never easy for deer in winter, even when their numbers are moderate. The herd on the plateau had grown to many thousands more deer than the food supply

Once launched in pursuit of its prey, the cheetah resembles a living blur. If several animals in a herd are startled into flight by the cat, it usually selects a specific individual as its target and pursues it to the exclusion of the others.

could support, especially in winter. More than half of the 100,000 deer had died of starvation by the spring of 1924.

When warm weather returned, the vegetation provided a renewed food source, but not for long. The remaining deer, and later the young born in the spring, devoured every scrap of vegetation they could find. They stripped the plateau almost bare, and when the food was gone they began to starve again. This grim chain of events continued for years.

In 1930, restrictions on hunting were eased. Natural predators also had begun to filter back into the area, although not in large numbers. Gradually the deer herd was reduced. Today, 10,000 deer are kept healthy on the plateau. The balance is maintained by artificial means, through careful management, not naturally as it was before war was waged against the cougars and other predators.

The cougar uses its sense of smell more than most other cats, sometimes tracking game by scent, but in hunting, the eyes and ears are still more important

than the nose. Once the prey is located, the cat begins a careful sequence of movements that bring it within about thirty feet of the intended victim. Flattening itself as low to the ground as it can, the cougar avoids sudden motion, which is likely to alarm its victim. If possible, it uses the cover of brush, fallen logs, or boulders, often detouring from a straight path to take advantage of the concealment. After moving from one spot to another, it may freeze momentarily, ever wary of frightening the prey. The cougar can remain so still that it can be in full view of a deer without being recognized.

Once in range, the cougar tenses, its muscular legs bunched under its body. Suddenly, like a spring that has snapped, the legs propel the animal over the ground toward its victim. The cat relies on the awesome impact of its 200-pound weight to overwhelm its prey, or at least to bowl it over. Unless caught almost immediately, the victim usually can escape, because although the cougar can run swiftly for several dozen yards, it tires quickly when sprinting. If the rush succeeds, the cougar sinks its foreclaws into the prey at the moment of contact, usually in the head or from behind, rather than on the flanks. Very small animals are likely to die in the cat's claws. Those of moderate size, such as deer, are bitten in the back of the neck. If the fangs do not end the victim's life, the cougar uses its grip to break the animal's neck.

102

The cougar's method of making a kill is generally similar to that used by most of the big cats, but there are variations, some observed only recently. The jaguar, for example, likes to wait in ambush, rather than stalk, and attacks its quarry from close range with a ferocious bound. (The name "jaguar" comes from an Indian word meaning a flesh-eater that "kills prey with one bound.")

The tiger's assault is designed to throw the prey off its feet—no easy job when the animal is as big as a gaur, which weighs about a ton and is the largest of wild cattle, or a water buffalo, which may be four times the tiger's weight. Despite their size, both animals are often hunted by tigers. As the victim goes down the tiger sinks its fangs into the neck. Holding the grip, the cat pins the victim, bracing itself on its elbows, chest close to the ground and hindquarters raised. The cat is so powerful that even the herculean efforts of gaur and buffalo to right themselves are usually vain, and they perish in the killer's jaws.

Increasingly, zoologists have observed that for most big cats the placement of the grip on the victim's neck seems to vary according to the prey's relative size. The tiger grabs deer by the nape, wild cattle by the throat. If during the initial assault on a big animal the tiger's teeth wind up in the back of the neck, the cat quickly shifts its grip to the throat once the prey falls. The leopard kills monkeys and baboons by biting through the nape, but it bites large antelopes in the throat. Snow leopards have been seen killing goats and sheep both by breaking the neck and by biting the throat. Lions also use both methods, with an apparent preference for the latter.

The reason for the different tactics seems to be that the nape of a large animal is protected by heavy slabs of muscle and a considerable amount of bone, making it difficult for the cat to deliver a lethal bite. By grabbing the throat, however, the cat can strangle its victim. The process is rarely quick—the downed animal may take several minutes to die. Lions also sometimes suffocate their victims by clamping their jaws over the snout, a method that does not kill any more swiftly than strangulation.

Some of the big cats occasionally hunt in small groups—a tiger and cubs, or a pair of courting leopards, for example—but they are for the most part solitary hunters. The one exception is the lion. A lion is perfectly capable of hunting on its own, but these tawny cats are known for their cooperative efforts.

Several members of a band, called a "pride," will join forces to catch antelope and similar game. While a few of the cats hide in the scrub or savannah grass, others herd the game toward them. The game may be driven slowly, or the herders may charge, sending the victims fleeing into the jaws of the ambushers.

A group of cheetahs (top) settles down to consume a kill. Although not as social as lions, cheetahs often band together to hunt. Lions and other scavengers are always eager to steal cheetah kills. Lions may drive cheetahs away, but vultures (bottom) take flight when chased by a cheetah.

105

Most of the hunting is done by the females. The males do much less, for one important reason—they do not really have to hunt for their food. The cooperativeness of the hunt does not carry over into the consumption of the meal. Then, it is every lion for itself. Bigger and stronger than the lionesses, the males take what they want. They need to hunt only when they cannot appropriate food from a female, or from another predator such as a hyena.

One of the other hunters com-

monly relieved of its kills by the lion is the cheetah, which, like the larger cat, seeks its prey among the grass and thorn scrub of the savannah. Both depend mainly on game herds—zebra and antelope of virtually all sizes. Like the cooperativeness of the lions, the dazzling speed of the cheetah provides a tremendous advantage in pursuing fleet hoofed animals out in the open. The cheetah is the fastest land animal, or, more accurately, the quickest over short distances.

For the first 500 yards of its sprint,

A tiger crouching in the grass provides a good example of how the striped coat of this great cat blends with its surroundings. Camouflage helps the tiger get in range of its prey, which it kills after making a short rush.

the cheetah sometimes reaches a speed of almost 70 miles an hour. That is more than enough to overtake a gazelle, which moves at about 45 miles an hour, if the cheetah can manage to stay with the antelope's twists and turns over the first several hundred yards. The cheetah expends so much energy in reaching its top speed that it tires rapidly. If the prey can keep out of the cat's reach for only the first few minutes of the chase, it is safe. The cheetah will be left standing, its flanks heaving with exhaustion. The cheetah therefore tries to conceal itself until it is within about 100 yards of its target. While it stalks, it watches every movement of the prey. The position of the eyes high on the skull enable the cheetah to see over the grass while the rest of its body stays close to the ground, a distinct advantage on the savannah.

As soon as it is close enough, the cheetah rockets out of concealment. As it runs, huge quantities of air are sucked through its extra-wide nostrils, bringing oxygen to its enlarged lungs. Its body

Tigers sometimes feed together at a kill. In such cases the animals usually are a mating pair or, as pictured here, a mother and offspring. On rare occasions male tigers also may permit a female with young to feed at their kill. Scientists have recently discovered that tigers are more sociable than was previously believed.

moves like a spring that is repeatedly flexed and released at speed. In slow motion, the stride would look like this: first the back is arched, hindquarters lowered, and feet pulled together, with rear limbs overlapping the front ones. Then the "spring" is released and the legs shoot out to their fullest extension, while the back sinks in concave fashion and the hindquarters thrust upward. All the while the long tail streams out behind.

The cheetah's doglike claws provide the traction it needs to follow the zigzags of its prey. If it can close in on a small antelope for only a moment, the cheetah, still running, tries to knock the animal's legs out from under it with a blow from a forepaw. A large animal such as a zebra is brought down with a more typically catlike leap. Like the lion and the tiger, the cheetah kills with a bite to the throat. Its jaws are too small and weak to make a fatal attack on the nape.

One of the prevalent misconceptions about the way big cats hunt is that they like to drop on their prey from overhanging limbs or ledges. A leopard or cougar sometimes will ambush an animal from above. Neither cat drops directly on the prey, however, but lands on the ground, then springs. The bobcat occasionally falls on quarry from above, but this is far from typical behavior. Of all the big cats, only the clouded leopard regularly hunts this way. The clouded leopard is known to seize deer and wild pigs by

falling on them from above, although because of the creature's secretive nature such attacks have seldom been witnessed. This small, beautifully marked cat of the Southeast Asian jungle also catches birds in its jaws, spiking them on its teeth.

Once a kill has been made, the big cats generally prefer to eat it in a quiet, secure place. If the prey has not been downed in such a location, the cat will move it to one. Big cats have the strength to lug animals of astonishing size about the countryside. Cougars regularly move deer weighing up to three times their own weight over distances of several dozen yards. Smaller animals, such as yearling deer weighing less than 100 pounds, have been transported by cats for more than a mile overland. Jaguars have crossed rivers with animals as big as horses. Cattle and buffalo that could not be moved by fewer than ten or twelve men have been dragged hundreds of feet by tigers, which may even leap for several yards while holding a carcass. Generally tigers drag their prey by the neck, but they have been seen carrying their victims over the shoulder. Because tigers like to soak in water during the heat of the day and frequently drink while eating, they often haul their prey to the banks of the nearest pool or stream, as long as there is enough brush there to provide cover. When both lions and tigers were widespread in Asia, the tigers' liking for water may have kept them out of more arid areas favored by lions.

Perhaps no big cat takes such pains to eat undisturbed as the leopard. Whenever a big cat makes a kill, a host of other beasts—especially wild dogs, hyenas, jackals, and other cats—gathers to steal a bite, or even to drive off the hunter. The leopard tries to avoid such unwelcome attention by stowing its victim in the branches of a tree and consuming it there at leisure. Some leopards repeatedly use the same tree as a dining platform. Leopards characteristically seize the head of a carcass in their jaws and carry it to one side, resting it along one flank, so that it is almost shouldered for extra support. The size of animals that even small leopards can carry into the branches is phe-nomenal. They have been seen taking animals more than twice their own weight dozens of feet above the ground.

The leopard eats according to a deliberate pattern. First it cuts open the belly of the carcass and removes the stomach and intestines, which it buries under grass, leaves, or dirt. Why it does this is hard to say, but by burying these parts the leopard removes some of the attractants for flies and other pesky insects. After eating the heart, liver, and kidneys, it consumes the forequarters of the carcass, and finally, if it is still hungry, the hindquarters.

The manner in which the prey is consumed varies, sometimes consider-

A jaguar walks its hunting range. The largest of the New World cats, the jaguar is extremely powerful and can bring down very large, often dangerous, victims.

ably, among the big cats. The cheetah, known as a messy eater, eats the heart and liver, then the flanks, and after that the ribs. Cheetahs customarily drink the blood that pools in the prey's body cavity. Drinking blood enables cheetahs to survive in the more arid parts of their range, where standing water is scarce.

Big cats can consume enormous amounts of food at one sitting. A single meal for a tiger, for example, may total one-fifth of its body weight, and it is not unknown for a tiger to bolt down more than 100 pounds of meat.

Since big cats do not eat every day, the total amount of food required over a prolonged period is consumed in periodic gorgings, usually spaced a few days apart. A cat does not have to kill a new animal every time it needs to eat. Most of the big cats can make several meals out of a single large victim. A few, however, including the cheetah and the bobcat, disdain all but fresh-killed meat.

More typical is the cougar. If it does not eat all of a kill, it covers the remains with vegetation and returns for more later. If there is anything left of a tiger's prey, the cat heaps leaves, grass, and earth over it. Grass may be bitten off in swatches and deposited. Or else the cat turns its back toward the carcass and sweeps earth and debris over it with a front paw. Tigers go so far as to shove carcasses between boulders to conceal them. Lions do not bury their kills but often re-

110

main in the shade near a large carcass, keeping interlopers off by their presence. They return repeatedly to eat, even after the meat has badly rotted.

Several of the big cats do not turn up their noses at carrion. Indeed, on occasion they may act more like scavengers than hunters. This is especially true of lions, which frequently get much of their food from animals killed by disease or by other predators. One lion followed for three weeks by a scientist got all its meals from victims killed by other animals. Cheetahs, leopards, and hyenas often are chased off their kills by lions. Hyenas once were believed to be cowardly pickers of the lion's leavings, but researchers who have watched both animals on the plains of East Africa have proved this a fallacy. Roving in packs, hyenas regularly surround and kill prey as large as zebras and wildebeests, the same type of creatures hunted by lions. Sometimes a single lion will put to flight a few hyenas and appropriate their kill. Conversely, large packs of hyenas often chase lions from carcasses, usually outnumbering them by about a dozen to one.

Tigers and leopards also are notorious eaters of carrion, even flesh that is badly decomposed. Sometimes a tiger will dig up the bodies of domestic animals that have been buried by their owners. There is one recorded case of a tiger digging up a cow carcass that had been dropped in a hole five feet deep and covered with a four-inch layer of dirt topped by heaps of thorn-studded branches.

Big cats sometimes travel great distances in search of food, especially if prey is scarce. During the low in the snowshoe hare's population cycle, the North American lynx sometimes wanders 100 miles in quest of sustenance. Tigers often patrol their neighborhood all night long, traveling more than a dozen miles while their keen eyes survey the darkness for victims. The progress of a tiger on the prowl often is heralded by sharp yips of alarm from the little muntjacs, or barking deer, that share the forests with the striped cat.

Cougars and leopards cover about the same distance while hunting as the tiger. When hunting, all of these big cats move at a pace that is steady but not particularly speedy—just two or three miles an hour, and often less than that.

Because they inhabit the open plains, lions have been observed more extensively than the large cats that live in dense forests or high mountains. On the savannahs of East Africa, each pride of lions stakes out its own hunting territory, sometimes 100 square miles.

Within its fief, the pride levies its toll on the great herds of wildebeest, Thompson's gazelle, and zebra that traverse it when the rainy season makes the plains lush. During this time, life is truly bounteous for the lions. They find abundant prey close at hand and live at ease.

A versatile hunter, the caracal takes a variety of prey. Top: This cat has killed an ibex, a wild goat that shares parts of its range in Africa and southern Asia. Bottom: Even venomous serpents are eaten by the caracal. The snake shown here is a dangerous sand viper.

113

Cougars often lie in ambush on ledges or tree limbs. They do not pounce directly on their victims, but jump to the ground and then chase after the prey. Often the prey is a deer, but the cougar also eats smaller animals.

When the rains cease, however, the herds migrate from the plains to more wooded areas where water and forage remain. The massing of the migratory herds, particularly the wildebeest, is an awesome sight. The dark bodies of the animals cover the flats and the rolling hillsides. The rumble of their passage sometimes seems to shake the air, and the night is filled with their snorts and grunts. Then, with remarkable abruptness, the huge assemblages of game are gone, leaving a landscape that looks denuded of grass.

During the wet season, Tanzania's Serengeti Plain is crowded with game. After the drought arrives, however, one can fly across the breadth of this region the size of Massachusetts and spot only isolated groups of animals—a few Grant's gazelles, an eland or two, and perhaps some topis. Flat to the horizon, the country looks dry and dusty, like a desert. In such lean periods, life is more difficult for the prides, and the cats must continually search to the limits of their territories to keep from starving. Yet only lone lions, no longer members of a pride, follow the migrating herds to their new pastures.

On the heights of central Asia, seasonal change prompts a migration of sorts by the snow leopard. In the summer, the cat roves near the roof of the world, at an altitude of almost 20,000 feet. There it finds the wild sheep and goats, particularly the great, spiral-horned markhor, that are its principal prey. When winter

storms blast the peaks, however, the game moves down the slopes. The markhor, for instance, spends the summer around and above the timber line, but winters in the deep, sheltered valleys, where it feeds on the evergreen foliage of the live oak. The snow leopard follows the goats in their migration, which may be only a few miles in actual distance but spans the same climatic zones as the migrations of birds that travel from the arctic tundra to temperate regions.

For cats from the cougar to the tiger, hoofed animals are the main prey. If the preferred victims are scarce, however, the cats turn to an astonishing variety of foods. A jaguar that cannot find peccaries, tapirs, or deer may leap into the water after quarry as rugged as the caiman, Central and South American relative of the alligator. Wild turkeys, monkeys, and capybaras—pig-size rodents—also serve the jaguar as food.

Tigers also look to the water when routine prey is unavailable. Those inhabiting the mangrove swamps of the Sundarbans on the Indian subcontinent regularly hunt fish in the tidal creeks. Throughout their range, tigers catch and kill creatures ranging from bears and badgers to lizards and porcupines.

Leopards in Africa are famed for tracking troops of baboons and picking off stragglers, and in Asia the spotted cats use the same tactics for killing macaques—like baboons, large ground-dwelling mon- 115

A bighorn ram careens down a mountain slope with a cougar in hot pursuit. Although the cougar is at home in the mountains, it cannot match the speed and sure-footedness of the ram on steep, rocky surfaces. The cat must be able to take the ram quickly, or it will lose its victim.

keys. In a pinch a lion will snap up a baboon, or almost any other animal it can handle. Driven by hunger, lions sometimes attack large, feisty creatures such as adult Cape buffalo and elephants, attacks that often result not in a meal but an empty stomach and broken bones.

Despite their great strength and stealth—tigers, for instance, have crept to within fifty feet of deer in grass six inches high without detection—the big cats often fail to capture the prey. Lions and tigers often go a week between meals. Some tigers observed by scientists for long periods failed on the majority of their hunts. Dr. George Schaller watched a tiger stalk a dozen times in an area where prey abounded. Only one attempt netted a meal for the tiger. Schaller estimates that tigers may have to make at least twenty attempts to catch an animal for every one that is successful.

Schaller has made similar observations of cats in Africa. He found that the success of the hunt depends largely on the condition of the prey and of the surrounding cover. Not surprisingly, cats end up with full bellies when they go after young or weak animals in heavy cover. The difference that these factors can make between hunger and a good meal is remarkable. A cheetah that was successful less than half the time when chasing adult Thompson's gazelles scored whenever the target was a fawn. When lions stalk gazelles in short grass, they miss

116

A bobcat and a snowshoe hare play a deadly game. Both are extremely agile, and both have wide, heavily furred paws that help them travel over snow. Hares, rabbits, and rodents make up a large part of the bobcat's diet.

five out of six times, but cut the odds to less than half in taller grass cover.

When game animals are depleted because of human activity, the big cats are in trouble, because their search for new food sources brings them into sharp conflict with man. The snow leopard that finds no more markhors in the valleys because the vegetation that the markhor eats has been stripped by domestic livestock turns to the stock for prey. In India, where the natural prey of the leopard has been eliminated from many areas, individuals often attach themselves to particular villages, making forays and snatching chickens, goats, and dogs, which are a favorite meal of leopards worldwide. Where domestic cattle have replaced the game herds in East Africa, lions readily feed on the cows, which are easier to catch than their warier wild counterparts.

Occasionally, some of the big cats seek out an even easier prey—man. This happens only rarely, but when a cat turns man-eater it can do so with a vengeance. Leopards are among the notorious man-eaters. The leopard of Panar, which terrorized a portion of northern India earlier in this century, destroyed four hundred people. The leopard of Rudraprayag, also in northern India, slaughtered more than a hundred human victims. Man-killing by leopards probably has gone on ever since people began to share the countryside with the spotted cats. In the skull of a young Australopithecine apeman who

Home is the hunter. A bobcat that has just completed a successful stalk carries a cottontail rabbit back to its lair. Bobcats are solitary hunters. Although most of their prey is small, they occasionally kill deer, especially old individuals or those that have become mired in deep snow.

lived in South Africa a million years ago scientists found two holes that seemed to be made by the fangs of a leopard as it dragged the body of its victim toward a tree. For a big cat of those times there probably was little difference between killing one of the baboons that roved the savannah and taking a member of the very similar troops of pre-humans who also wandered the plains.

Tigers that for one reason or another take a liking to human flesh also have terrorized entire regions. This is true not only for the past, but even today. Studies made in the Sundarbans region of India, long noted for producing man-eat-

ers, showed that almost three hundred humans were killed by tigers between 1961 and 1971. In 1975, a tiger jumped into a boat carrying people on a river in Thailand and nearly killed a passenger before it was driven away. Late in 1978, authorities had to kill a tiger that had eaten seven people in an area about 500 miles east of New Delhi.

Lions, too, continue to take a toll of humans, although the number of victims is restricted to a handful. Every year or so, however, there are reports of people being killed by supposedly unprovoked lions in Africa. None of these incidents compares for sheer terror with the murderous raids carried out by man-eating lions of the past, the most infamous of which were the two killers of Tsavo, in southeastern Kenya.

The so-called Man-eaters of Tsavo appeared just before the turn of the century and began to seize workers building a railroad near the Tsavo River. The lions caused such terror that work on the line was halted. The British government, ruling Kenya as a colony, ordered the destruction of the lions, which eventually was accomplished with extreme difficulty and danger by Colonel J. H. Patterson, a hunter and engineer who was helping construct the railroad.

None of the other big cats can be considered a man-eater, although there have been one or two instances of cougars eating people, and jaguars certainly have the power, if not the inclination, to do so. What makes man-eaters is a mystery. Over the years myriad explanations have been proposed. Inability to catch more active prey, because of illness or wounds, is one suggestion. Unknown changes in the internal chemistry of the killers is another, as is the possibility that some cats become addicted to human flesh after eating the bodies of dead people, especially during epidemics or wars, when corpses are abundant.

Finding an answer has become especially important in recent years, as the numbers of big cats dwindle, and those that remain find themselves in proximity to increasing human populations. In the early 1970s the World Wildlife Fund sponsored a study by a German scientist, Dr. Hubert Hendricks, which may help clear up the mystery.

Hendricks went to the Sundarbans, where the seaside forest is the haven for a large number of tigers, and at the same time is used for many human endeavors, chiefly logging and honey-gathering. He found that some tigers never attack people, even when alarmed, but that others are aggressive to a varying degree, although not really predatory toward humans. Only 3 percent of the tigers in the region could be considered real man-eaters, that is, those that deliberately hunt people. Some of these may have become man-eaters after killing humans who disturbed them, and then acquiring a taste for their flesh. Interestingly, the study also showed that attacks on man increased when the sea flooded the region, which is a large delta. Under such conditions, much of the tiger's normal prey would disappear. A return to normal water levels was paralleled by a decrease in assaults by the tigers.

Learning about the relationships between the big cats and the animals on which they feed has always been important to understanding these magnificent animals. It is of critical importance today, when the survival of the big cats, even in the remotest of places, depends ultimately on human tolerance.

4

big cats are born with a hunter's instincts. They arrive in the world not only with the desire to stalk and make a kill, but also with the innate abilities necessary to accomplish this task. This is not to say that at birth they possess all the knowledge needed to capture prey—far from it. A newborn cat has much to learn, many skills to acquire and polish, before it can be an effective hunter. All the skills gained through experience, however, are built on a foundation of inborn responses, of behavior patterns that do not have to be learned, but occur naturally when provoked by cues in the environment.

No cub or kitten has to be taught the basic form of the stalk, it only has to learn to do it well. When a young lion sees an object that it instinctively senses is a game animal, it will begin herding it toward the other members of the pride, not by conscious plan, but because of inherited responses. Big cats are born killers.

The strength of inherited hunting behavior in the big cats is demonstrated by what happened when a zoo curator brought home a six-week-old cougar cub that had been removed by conservation authorities from a roadside animal show. It had been nursed back to health by the zoo veterinarian and was accustomed to being handled. When an educational television program asked the curator to bring a wild cat to the studio, the cougar cub was selected. It was taken to the curator's home for the night so he could bring it directly to the studio in the morning.

Immediately, the curator's two-and-a-half-year-old son found the cat a perfect playmate. Since the cub, no larger than a big house cat, could do no damage as long as it was watched, the curator let the boy and the cat romp together in the living room. The youngster ran back and forth, and the cat chased after him. The chasing was not aimless. It quickly became apparent that the cub's play mirrored the basic stalk-and-kill technique that, if it were wild, it would use to gain a living as an adult. When the boy scampered by, the cub raced in pursuit, closing quickly from a yard or so away. Pulling alongside the tot, the cub would rear up on its hind legs in approximation of a spring. Its forepaws would land on the youngster's shoulders, pulling him down, while it nipped with its tiny teeth at the back of the boy's neck—not nearly hard enough to break the skin, or even bruise it, but enough to make the child squeal. The cub was performing the typical nape bite used by adult cougars to kill deer. It had hardly known its mother, and had spent almost all its life in the exclusive company of humans. It was clumsy and often missed its target while the boy ran and wrestled with it, but the basic cougar hunting behavior had obviously been part

124

**Preceding pages:
From its perch in a
tree, a young lion
cub surveys the East
African savannah.
By watching the adult
lions hunt, cubs
begin to learn
survival skills while
still very young.
Left: Tiger cubs enjoy
mock battles. Such
play sessions
strengthen the cubs'
muscles and give
them an opportunity
to practice moves
that will help them
survive as adults.**

of it since birth.

On its own in the wild, however, the cougar cub would not have survived. It would need much more than its inherited hunting instinct to fill its belly and avoid falling prey to another hunter. Growth is not merely the development of size and strength. A young big cat must learn essential skills from its mother and others of its kind, and gain experience through its encounters with nature.

The more complex a creature is, the longer it takes for it to mature. Time is needed to develop the strengths, skills, and social relationships necessary for survival. The actual length of "childhood," of course, is relative to the life span of the creature. Bobcats, which have a life expectancy of about a decade, are born in spring and are on their own by autumn. The leopard, which in captivity lives more than twenty years, leaves home after about a year.

A big cat begins life isolated from the rest of the world, except for its mother. During gestation—three months for a cougar, almost four for a tiger, two for a lynx—the mother is the entire world of the mammalian embryo. For mammals that are born helpless, such as cats, this

125

Lion cubs are weaned at six or seven months. Their permanent teeth erupt between the ninth and twelfth month, causing pain and restlessness, sometimes accompanied by fever. During this period the death rate among cubs is high. Those that survive begin to act more independently, but remain with their mother for about two more years.

complete dependency persists for a time even after birth.

Being born in the dry season (as the lion is) or in the spring (as the cougar is) is an advantage for the cubs from an evolutionary standpoint. By the time the lion cubs have cut their teeth, the rains have arrived, turning the grass lush. The game herds are returning from their seasonal migration to the woodlands, and there is meat aplenty for the cubs, especially since the herd animals themselves are bearing young—a source of highly vulnerable prey. In the temperate zones, the same applies to cats born in the spring. By late spring the prey animals also have

borne young, and thus the amount of food available to the cats increases significantly.

The nursery in which the big cat is born varies, but it is always away from the crowd. The mother must have solitude during the vulnerable period in which she is giving birth. The bobcat mother-to-be selects a den in a hollow log, perhaps under the roots of a large tree, or in a small cave. Sometimes bobcats have their young in tree hollows several feet above the ground. The adaptable leopard also uses a variety of sites, from rocky caves to hollow trees. The lynx looks for a shelter in the brush, making little preparation

other than tamping down the vegetation. The caracal uses natural heaps of rotting vegetation, rock shelters, or even vacant burrows of other animals. The female ocelot finds a hollow log, cave, or similar shelter when she is ready to give birth. She lines the interior of this nursery with soft vegetation and hair. Cougars usually are born in caves or rock shelters. Jaguars, lions, and cheetahs give birth in thickets, although sometimes the cheetah makes do with a natural bower of tall grass. Clouded leopards give birth in standing hollow trees. The tiger sometimes uses thickets, or else dens up beneath a hollow log or perhaps among a jumble of rocks.

The snow leopard bears its young in a cave or under a ledge, after lining the cavity with its own fur, which provides insulation against the rigorous elements of its mountain habitat.

Little is known about the early life of the snow leopard in the wild, because of the remoteness of its home. Several zoos, however, have bred a number of these beautiful animals. Among the most successful has been the Bronx Zoo, which in 1978 videotaped the birth of two snow leopard cubs, eventually named Pete and Rose after the well-known baseball player then with the Cincinnati Reds. (The cubs' father was on loan to the Bronx

Opposite: Lion cubs in Lake Manyara National Park, Tanzania, eat a young wart hog. Cubs begin to accompany their mother on hunting expeditions when they are about three months old. Left: Bonds between mother and young are strong during the first few months of the cubs' life. Here, a lioness and her cub share a tender moment.

institution from the Cincinnati Zoo.)

The tape showed the mother lying quietly in the dark recesses of the enclosure's holding area, a good approximation of a cave. She moved very little as she was giving birth. Shortly after the cubs were born, she began to nuzzle and lick them, a process that serves not only to cleanse the babies but also to stimulate their bodily functions, such as circulation and defecation. Moments after that, she consumed the afterbirth.

Totally blind, the cubs nevertheless sensed the warmth of their mother and crawled toward her, burrowing into her soft fur. Their complete helplessness was obvious—they could not even walk. With most big cats, the cubs' activity begins to increase only when their eyes open. Although some cats in zoos have been born with eyes open, it normally is several days before the cubs can see. Lynxes, bobcats, caracals, cougars, leopards, and snow leopards generally open their eyes before they are a week and a half old. Clouded leopards, jaguars, tigers, and cheetahs usually are nearer a week old when this occurs. Lion cubs sometimes stay blind for as long as three weeks after birth.

Few animals appear as cute and cuddly as the cubs of wild cats. For this 129

Cubs of the big cats are always spotted or striped. The markings serve as protective coloration, helping to hide the cubs from predators. Despite the camouflage, many young cubs are killed. Right: Cheetah cubs. Opposite top: Young leopard. Opposite bottom: Lion cubs.

reason, a number of wild cats have earned the admiration of pet fanciers, and in recent years a number of these animals have been brought into people's homes, especially as cubs. This is an unsound practice, both for the welfare of the cats and for their human owners. Wild cats are always dangerous as they grow. They have not been subjected to thousands of generations of domestic breeding, as domestic cats have. Many pet owners have been hurt, and some have been killed, by wild cats. The trade in wild pets, moreover, has been a significant factor in the decline of a number of wild cat species. If a person truly admires and cares about wild felines, the last thing he or she should do is try to keep them as pets.

Most of the big cats have between two and four young per litter. Occasionally, however, there are more. Snow leopards have had as many as five cubs. Leopards, jaguars, and cougars have been known to produce as many as a half-dozen young in a single litter. Tigers may have seven, and lions and cheetahs occasionally eight or nine. As a rule, however, the survival to adolescence of two cubs out of a single litter is considered a healthy rate.

All big cats, whether or not they are striped or spotted as adults, are born with markings on their coats. Caracal cubs have reddish spots on their undersides. Cougar cubs are heavily marked with black spots and have very dark ears;

130

131

they also have rings on their tails, which are much more rounded than the tails of the adults. By the time the cougar is about six months old, the spots have vanished, except for a dark tail tip, which remains permanently. Young lions also have spots, even stripes, which sometimes last, albeit faintly, almost into adulthood. The adults retain only dark patches behind the ears, similar to those of the tiger.

It is tempting to speculate about the evolutionary significance of the spots (or stripes) that virtually all wild cats are born with. Are the markings a throwback to the remote ancestors of today's felines? Perhaps the original feline stock was spotted. It is possible that most prehistoric cats were marked like the leopard, jaguar, and cheetah. It is entirely feasible that the great cat that coursed over the plains of North America, and the saber-tooths that preyed on the beasts caught in the tar pits at La Brea, had spotted coats. Depictions of the ancient cave lion found on cavern walls in Europe seem to indicate that the cat was spotted as an adult.

Even among the cats with markings that persist throughout life, there are differences in the coloration of the young. The faces of jaguar cubs are striped with black at birth. As the youngsters grow the stripes break up into solid spots. In addition, young jaguar cubs' coats are of a browner cast than those of the adults. The spots on cheetah cubs are smaller than those of the adults, while those on young

A lioness, nursing a cub, warns off a second youngster. Lionesses sometimes discipline their cubs quite forcefully, especially when the playful youngsters become mischievous. Usually, though, lionesses are very affectionate with the cubs in their pride.

133

leopards are ill-defined, hiding the ground color.

Among most of the big cats, color mutations occasionally occur—individuals are born with strikingly atypical coloration for their species. Especially in India and Southeast Asia, melanistic, or black, leopards are sometimes born. There is a popular misconception that these leopards are another type of cat, the so-called black panther, which is supposedly craftier, more powerful, and more savage than the run-of-the-mill leopard.

Such beliefs are balderdash. The "black panther" is just a color phase, or variety, of the standard leopard species, nothing more or less. No extra strength, agility, or savagery goes with the dark color. Some researchers believe that the black coat may be more difficult to see in the shadows of a forest, and thus constitute an advantage for animals living there, but even this has never been successfully documented.

The entire myth of the "black panther" as a superleopard or a distinct creature is invalidated when it is remembered that the black variety is usually born with spotted litter mates. The gene that gives rise to melanism is recessive,

Newborn cheetahs are yellow-gray in color, with a long, light gray mane running down the neck and back. The mane is lost by the time the cubs are ten weeks old, and the coat gradually becomes pale yellow, the color of the grass in which cheetahs often lie.

so the dark cub, or cubs, usually are outnumbered by ordinary siblings. Furthermore, if one looks closely at the coat of a black leopard, very faint spots can be seen. The same is true of black jaguars, which while uncommon may be born more frequently than melanistic leopards. Most black jaguars come from the Amazon, the heart of the jaguar's range. Melanism also occurs among cougars, but much less frequently than among jaguars and leopards.

Albinism is seldom found among the big cats. When it does occur, it may not be real absence of color but merely a light phase. This is true of the so-called white tigers exhibited by some zoos. White tigers are occasionally observed in the wild in India and in several other parts of Asia. Those in zoos should be considered freaks created through purposeful breeding that has concentrated the genes responsible for the color in a few lines of animals. Such tigers are blue-eyed, black-striped, with a white (sometimes yellow-tinged) background color. While their coloration makes these creatures popular curiosities in zoos, it is almost certainly a distinct disadvantage in the wild, where a white tiger would be all too highly vis-

ible. Zoos that perpetuate white tigers would do better to breed the normal variety, which needs all the help it can get to avoid extinction.

The size of big cats at birth ranges from slightly less than a pound to about three pounds. The most accurate weight measurements for cubs come from zoos, which can weigh the animals shortly after they are born. Not surprisingly, the largest of the big cats—tigers, lions, and jaguars—have the biggest young, usually between two and three pounds. The cubs generally are about a foot and a half long, including the tail. Leopards and cougars usually are a little more than a pound at birth. The smallest of the big cats, the bobcat, often comes into the world weighing slightly less than a pound.

Suckled on mother's milk, big cat cubs grow rapidly, even in the first days of life. Some records at the Bronx Zoo demonstrate this very graphically. A lion cub born in 1944 that weighed three pounds at birth had more than doubled its weight within fifteen days. In about two and a half months it was the size of some adult bobcats—17 pounds. Nine months after it was born, the cub had reached 99 pounds. Rajpur, a male tiger born the same year, weighed two pounds, nine ounces at birth. Nine days later its weight was four pounds. At nine months it was 147 pounds, and shortly before its second birthday, the cat had reached 438 pounds and was still growing.

A similar rate of growth was recorded for a jaguar at the zoo. It was the sole male in a litter of three cubs born at the Bronx institution in April, 1954. After a few days, the cubs were taken from their mother, who was showing signs of nervousness, and given to a member of the zoo's staff to rear. On the day they were removed, the male weighed in at two pounds, fourteen and a half ounces. Within two weeks it had gained a pound, and after a month it weighed more than five pounds. By the end of the summer it was more than 24 pounds. Several weeks before its second birthday, the young jaguar was weighed again. It was almost 167 pounds, the size of a big leopard or cougar, and was still growing.

Opposite: Cheetah cubs stand atop a termite mound in the Samburu Game Reserve of Kenya. In doing this, they appear to imitate their elders, who use high vantage points to look out over the plains for prey. Left: Young cheetahs begin to hunt by catching small animals like the dove being eaten here.

The cats begin to cut their milk teeth within a few weeks after birth. Tiger cubs begin at about ten or eleven days; lions take about a week longer. The time at which cubs are weaned also differs slightly among species, although they begin to taste meat weeks or even months before switching to it exclusively. Bobcats start chewing on flesh at the age of four weeks, at least a month before they are weaned. The clouded leopard begins sampling meat at six weeks. Leopards, lions, and tigers sometimes begin to eat bits of meat before they are two months old, but continue to suckle for about two months longer. At about a month and a half, cougar cubs begin to eat scraps of meat and to try out their teeth on the bones of prey killed by their mother.

By the time the young are ready for weaning, their mother—and in some species their father as well—is busy hunting food for them. Paternal participation in rearing the young is not common to all cats, and indeed it varies even within a single species. The female leopard, for example, sometimes tolerates the presence of the male around the young, and the male reciprocates by helping catch prey. He also serves as an extra guard for the youngsters.

When a bobcat has a litter, she keeps the male at a distance, but once the young begin to yowl for meat she may allow him to be a provider. Once in a great while, the male cheetah also helps

These young cheetahs in Tanzania's Serengeti National Park are learning hunting skills at the side of their mother. Females have been observed bringing live prey to their young, giving the cubs an opportunity to practice making a kill. The cubs' early attempts at bringing down prey are often quite clumsy.

139

Unlike adult cheetahs, young cubs can climb trees. Their claws are still retractable because they have not yet lost the claw sheaths with which they were born. The sheaths begin to degenerate when the cubs are about fifteen weeks old. Young cheetahs seen in trees are often confused with young leopards like the one shown opposite.

raise the cubs. Generally, however, by the time the cubs are capable of following their mother on short treks about the countryside, he is not involved in their care.

Cheetahs are weaned quickly, sometimes in two months, and by then they have begun to travel with their mother, seldom denning in the same place for more than a day. While she hunts, the cubs stay in the brush, supposedly hidden, although often their rambunctiousness gets the better of them and they gambol about, even climbing into low thorn scrub. They are able to climb easily because their claws are retractable until they are about six months old. When the cubs are very small, the female

brings the prey to them. She sometimes removes all the skin and consumes it, so the little teeth of the youngsters do not have to cope with the tough hide. As soon as the cubs are fairly mobile, the mother stays with the kill and summons the young, which respond quickly—both because they run as fast as their small legs can manage and because the female hunts close to where she has left them. Often the kill is made within a few hundred yards of the den.

The call used by the cheetah to rouse the youngsters has been described as a soft chirp. Similarly, the tigress issues a low grunt when summoning her young from hiding to come to a kill. Tiger cubs are kept in a permanent den for a

month or two. After that, they follow their mother throughout her hunting range. While she prowls, they hide in vegetation such as tall grass or thickets. If the kill is nearby, she may call the cubs over. Otherwise she approaches them and grunts softly several times. Tiger cubs respond to these grunts by following their mother if she is walking, or by coming to her if she is resting near a kill.

The lioness also grunts to keep her cubs in line. They begin needing management when they are about six weeks old. Until then, they stay in and around the secluded den in which they were born, sometimes remaining alone for an entire day while their mother hunts. Within a few weeks, however, they become bundles of energetic curiosity, and the lioness brings them from the den to join the rest of the pride. They meet the other cubs and their mothers, which share some of the responsibilities of rearing the young. If one lioness goes off hunting, the others watch over her brood and may even suckle them.

The lions' cooperativeness—also evident when they hunt—vanishes once the game is downed. Prey killed by any member of the pride is available to all,

Opposite: Caracal mother and cubs. Left: Ocelot cub. Caracals differ from ocelots in habits as well as appearance. Ocelots live primarily in forests and thickets and are generally quite shy. Caracals, considerably fiercer than ocelots, usually dwell in open country.

but this does not mean that it is shared equitably. Instead, every pride member grabs what it can, and solicitous behavior disappears, even with regard to the cubs. Especially if the victim is small and provides insufficient meat to go around, mealtime is accompanied by snarling, baring of teeth, and, not infrequently, blows. Cubs and elderly lions often must be content with only scraps. Even a cub's own mother will not willingly share her portion of the repast.

The tigress, on the other hand, feeds her cubs unselfishly, although she snarls if one of her offspring attempts to steal a piece from under her nose. Sometimes the tigress and cubs will permit a male to share the carcass, if he feeds peacefully and presents no threat. Usually, however, the female will warn him off, and she seldom has to resort to anything more vigorous than a long, hard stare.

If the prey is large—a gaur weighing a ton, for example—the tiger cubs and mother may remain with it for several days. By and large they will stay hidden a short distance from the carcass, returning to it periodically and eating until it is consumed. George Schaller observed this

143

During the heat of the day, the female tiger and her young remain hidden in the shade of the forest, often cooling themselves in the nearest pool of water. Though they range throughout the Asian tropics, tigers are northern in origin and do not like heat.

sort of behavior while studying the relationships between tigers and their prey in the Kanha National Park of India. The victim was an adult gaur bull, which had been dispatched by a tigress in a ravine. For five days between periodic meals, the tigress and cubs rested in the grass, 110 feet away from the carcass, or just out of sight around a bend in the gully. Often, while the mother dozed, the cubs played nearby.

The cougar family behaves in similar fashion, with mother and young leaving the den and wandering the countryside as the mother hunts. When she brings down a large victim, they camp near the carcass and feed periodically until there is nothing edible left. The mother always keeps a wary eye on the cubs, even as they run and play.

Early childhood is fraught with perils for the young of even the most ferocious cats. Unless they have constant protection, the young hunters may become the victims of other killers. The jungles that are the home of the clouded leopard, for example, are also the hunting grounds of one of the world's largest snakes, the reticulated python, said to reach a length of thirty-five feet. Certainly this creature, as well as smaller pythons of the region, would not turn down a meal of clouded leopard cubs discovered untended in a tree hollow. These snakes undoubtedly also menace the cubs of tigers and leopards within their range.

144

Tiger cubs weigh about two and a half pounds at birth. By the time they are four months old they are as large as a good-size dog, and they are almost full-grown at sixteen months. The cubs begin to eat meat when they are six weeks old. At this time they begin to leave the den and follow their mother to kills.

The big spotted hyenas of Africa, which are extremely powerful and sometimes run in large packs, take a toll of untended big cat cubs—caracals, leopards, lions, and cheetahs. According to zoologist Randall Eaton, a cat specialist who observed cheetahs in East Africa in 1966 and 1967, predation on cubs by hyenas may be a major influence on the number of cheetahs in the wild. Hyenas, especially in gangs, sometimes even kill adult big cats.

Another enemy of young cheetahs, and sometimes of adults, is the Cape hunting dog, which courses after game on the African savannah. Hunting in organized packs, and using such sophisticated tactics as decoy techniques, the wild dogs are efficient killers, on occasion even menacing adult lions and leopards. To decoy prey, a few members of the pack make themselves very obvious, thereby distracting the victim, while several other dogs, unseen, sneak up on it.

The Asian counterparts of the African hunting dogs are the "red dogs," or dholes. The dhole, as its nickname implies, is reddish in color. It is about 22 inches high at most, and a large male may reach more than 40 pounds in weight. In general appearance, it resembles the pariah dogs, the domestic curs that laze around villages and towns throughout southern Asia. The most obvious difference between the two is in the tail. The pariah's tail is curled, whereas the dhole's

is straight. Dholes live over a wide area. The northern boundary of their range is in central Asia, as far north as Manchuria. From there they range through India and Indochina through the Malay Archipelago.

As a rule, dholes hunt in packs. The members of the pack act as relay teams to chase their prey until it tires. The sight of dholes making a kill is especially gruesome, for they can literally tear a victim to pieces while they are running it. The dogs are swift enough to keep pace with deer, snapping and biting as they run. The scourge of game, dholes also have been known to kill adult leopards and tigers. A savage battle between a female tiger and a dhole pack was witnessed in the 1950s. About a half-dozen dogs in an advance contingent from the main pack had surrounded the tigress. The dogs attacked her just as they do big game. When she charged one of them, another would snap at her from behind, so she was kept busy from all sides. Suddenly the tigress heard the calls of the main pack, almost a score of animals, closing in. She charged one of the dogs and broke its spine with a great whack of her paw. Then she spurted away, with the advance dogs behind her, followed a few minutes later by the entire pack. The chase covered five miles, until the pack finally cornered the tigress, overpowered her, and ate her.

It is easy to see that predators

such as red dogs are a danger to big cat cubs. Actually, most carnivores except for the smallest species will kill and eat young cats if given the opportunity. So will a number of large birds, such as eagles and vultures, which are especially abundant in Africa. Though vultures are mainly scavengers, these birds treat helpless cubs like dying animals and consume them.

In North America the great horned owl, silent hunter of the forest, preys on unattended young bobcats. There are many North American mammalian predators that are of sufficient size and strength to kill young wild cats, and in some instances they challenge even the adults. The wolverine or glutton, a large, powerful member of the weasel family with strength and courage that is legendary in the north woods, has driven adult cougars from their prey. An often-overlooked danger to both young and adult cats—and to many other animals as well—is the domestic dog. Packs of free-running dogs, both strays and pets that have been let loose, rove most rural areas in the United States, killing countless wild animals. They pose a definite hazard to the wild cats. Grizzly bears, black bears, coyotes, and wolves also have the size and inclination to prey on the cubs of any cats left alone by their mothers. Wolves also have killed full-grown cougars.

Wolves share some of the territory inhabited by the Eurasian lynx, snow leopard, leopard, and tiger. So do a number of big bears—the brown, Asian black, and sloth bears. Though records of predation by such creatures on young big cats are sparse, they all are potential dangers.

The big cats not infrequently prey on one another, and not only young are taken. Adult caracals and cheetahs are sometimes felled and eaten by leopards, and all three can be victimized by lions. The cubs, of course, even of lions, are much more vulnerable. George Schaller observed a leopard kill a lion cub that had been left by its mother while she went off to get her other offspring. The lioness had killed a wildebeest, eaten part of it, and then went to find her cubs, which she had left hidden about a mile away. The cubs were young, and had to be carried in the mother's mouth. She hauled one of them over to the kill, which had been appropriated by a leopard during her absence. Seeing her approach, the spotted cat ascended a tree and waited. The lioness dropped her cub by the carcass, and then seemed seized with uncertainty—she set out after her second, only to return after taking a few strides. Finally she went off again. When she had gotten about a hundred yards away, the leopard dropped to the ground and seized the cub. As soon as the cub cried out, the lioness rushed back and drove off the leopard, but she was too late to save her youngster.

Cougars occasionally kill bobcats,

148

and tigers in Siberia and Manchuria prey on lynxes. Leopards also fall victim to tigers. Over the years, several reports of cannibalism among tigers also have been authenticated. In fact, not only tigers, but leopards, jaguars, and lions all are known to turn cannibal on occasion.

Episodes of cannibalism are rare, however, and seem to occur more frequently among lions than other cats. From time to time, in places as far apart as Kenya and South Africa, cannibalism breaks out among lions. Generally only a few individuals are involved. Sometimes the attacks take place within the pride, but more often they occur when males from one pride find unguarded cubs from another. Males have been seen attacking the leader of another pride, vanquishing him, then killing and eating the cubs. Such instances, however, are extremely uncommon, especially where prides have sufficient territories to themselves.

Predation, abandonment, starvation, disease, and a host of other perils make growing up a difficult time for the young big cats. Normally, only half the cubs born to a pride survive to young

149

Jaguar cubs. Young jaguars hunt with their mother until they are about two years old. They reach sexual maturity at the age of three years, but continue to grow until they are almost four. Except during the mating season, adult jaguars are not sociable.

adulthood. As the young cats mature, they acquire all the learned behavior that, when coupled with instinctive responses, enables them to join the society of their species. Whether or not a cat is social—as the lion is—it lives within the context of a feline society, with rules peculiar to its own kind. The rules, by and large, are learned long before adulthood.

The education that enables a big cat to play an active part in the society of its species begins literally at the moment of birth. At this point the first bonds are formed between the cub and others of its kind—initially its mother, then its siblings. These bonds are not automatic. They are created and reinforced by an in-

terplay of behavior between the animals they link. With a newborn mammal, such as a cat, the first forging of bonds begins with the scent, warmth, and touch experienced by both mother and young.

As it enters the world, a cub's first sensations are involved with the smells and surfaces around it—the rough but tender touch of the mother's tongue, her soft, warm presence, the dark security of the den. Already the process by which the cub learns to recognize its own kind has begun. For now it focuses on the smell of the mother, as she does on that of her offspring. Quickly recognition will be extended to the litter mates, perhaps even to the nursery itself, and eventually to

others of its species. During the first months of life, the most important function of these bonds is to cement the small family of mother and young together, and thus promote their survival.

The first bonds are formed unconsciously, as a by-product of actions that the mother instinctively performs to help the newborn start functioning on its own. By licking and nosing the young, to clean it and to prod its bodily processes into increased activity, the mother is also building her attachment to the cub, and its to her. When the cub begins to nurse, mutual attachment again is fostered by the utter dependence of the cub and the mother's urge to care for and protect it.

During the first few weeks of life, the young need almost constant attention from the mother. As the cubs mature, dependency begins to decrease, at first so slightly it can hardly be detected. The length of time the young need their mother in order to survive varies considerably among the different species. The clouded leopard, like the bobcat, the caracal, and the lynx, leaves its mother after nine or ten months. Leopard and snow leopard families break up about a year after the young are born. Adolescents of most other species have a reasonably good chance of surviving on their own after they reach a year of age, but the odds improve immeasurably when they remain

151

with their mothers for two years or longer. Occasionally tiger cubs remain as long as four years.

As soon as the young have cut their milk teeth and gained mobility, their real education commences. From then on, under the tutelage of their mother, they learn to hunt. By this time, the cubs have been playing at hunting with considerable verve. Siblings, insects, small birds, and blown leaves all are targets for a playful stalk and rush. Young cheetahs, not yet old enough for hunting lessons, sometimes even chase jackals that skulk about the carcasses of prey killed by the adults.

Schooling becomes serious for cheetah cubs when they are about four months old. At first the mother may catch young victims alive, carry them to the cubs, and release them for her offspring to chase. Until they grow and learn from experience, the cubs often fail to accomplish the job, and the mother must intervene at some point. One female cheetah was seen carrying a struggling gazelle fawn to her cubs. Once she released it the youngsters managed to knock it down, but it was too strong for them, and their mother had to kill it.

Another tactic used by the female cheetah is to lead her cubs to young or small victims, and then let them take over the hunt. A female was observed using this method to instruct her offspring at the expense of some wart hogs. With the cubs creeping belly-down behind her, the female stalked to within striking distance of a sow and her two very small young. Then the female charged, the cubs sprinting behind her. Obviously, her object was not to kill a wart hog immediately, but to separate the sow from the young. The adult wart hog is armed with sharp tusks and has the strength and will to use them. Undistracted, therefore, the sow would have made short work of the cubs.

On this occasion, however, the sow could not reach the cubs, because the female cheetah harassed her and finally drove her away. Meanwhile, the cubs ran after the small pigs, easily catching up with them. The cubs and their prey galloped in wide circles, but the young cheetahs seemed not to know how to bring down the pigs. The mother cheetah, moreover, made no move to help. Both young wart hogs escaped.

Young leopards learn to stalk by creeping behind their mother, then following her when she explodes in her final rush. At first, the cubs are seldom alert enough to charge simultaneously with their parent, but gradually their agility and reactions are sharpened. Instead of following their mother, young lynxes fan out in a feline approximation of a skirmish line and attempt to flush their game from the brush.

Since lions often hunt close to the pride and on open plains rather than in

The most common wild feline in the United States, the bobcat generally has two to four young. After giving birth, the female drives the male away, but he usually stays in the area. When the cubs are ready to eat solid food, the male may help obtain it for them.

153

Cougars are born in a well-concealed den, sometimes situated between boulders. In warm climates, cougars may give birth at any time of year; in cold climates, the young are usually born between April and June. The female lines the den with moss, leaves, and her own fur. The cubs are as playful as domestic kittens.

heavy forest, the cubs have a good view of what is happening. Before the cubs have reached three months of age, they have started to learn by watching. By their third month they begin to tag along with the hunters. Some cubs may go along for part of the hunt, then stay behind and watch. The more adventurous cubs may stick close to the lionesses as they stalk.

Only when the young lions are completing their sixth month of life do they participate in the entire stalk, and even then they seldom take part in the actual kill. Not until they are close to a year old do the cubs really contribute to the group effort in the hunt. By that time they have learned enough to help drive game, and even to lend their strength, fangs, and claws to bringing down big animals. Lion cubs seldom make kills on their own, however, until a few months after their first birthday. Biologist Schaller says he has never seen a cub under fifteen months hunt and kill on its own.

A similar pattern of development is seen in the tiger cub. By the time it is about six months old it is completely weaned and is starting to mimic its mother's hunting behavior. While their mother relaxes, the cubs may prowl about a short distance away, going through the motions of stalking. Within a few months they may be capable of catching small animals like peafowl by themselves. For the most part, however, they continue to

hunt with their mother.

Even when the cubs are a year old and weigh about 200 pounds, they are not yet skilled or strong enough to take prey as large as gaur or big domestic cattle. Their mother is still teaching them. In many instances she will down a large victim and, instead of polishing it off (as she could easily do), will disable it and hold it down for her cubs to attack. The manner in which adolescent tigers assault such a victim shows that they need considerable practice before they master the technique of killing a big animal. They do not try for the throat bite that kills by strangulation. Instead, the cubs torment the victim, although not purposely. They bite and claw virtually any area of exposed flesh they can, and if the mother manages to hold the prey down, they often begin to devour it alive. The prey may suffer for an hour or two before it dies.

As their skills grow, the cubs may help in capturing, if not killing, large animals. In one tiger family that was observed hunting, the cubs circled a buffalo, then attacked en masse. They bowled it over so that the female, standing nearby, could kill it.

Like the lion, the tiger learns the technique of biting the throat of large prey by the time it is about eighteen months old. Even then, the cub may have difficulty handling the task alone, so the longer it remains with its parent, the bet-

154

A young cougar awaits its dinner. Cougar cubs can eat meat at six weeks of age. The mother brings them small prey such as birds, rabbits, and squirrels. The father does not participate at all in raising the young.

ter chance it has of surviving. Each time the cub hunts on its own, however, it is setting the stage for its departure and commencement of adult life. Just as bonds are built by a succession of activities by parent and young, the ties that hold a feline family together are severed one link at a time.

Breaking of the bonds really begins even before the cubs are weaned. Every time a cub strays a short distance from the den, bonds are weakened. Changes are very slight at first, but they become increasingly meaningful as time passes. The farther the cub goes, and the longer it stays away, the weaker the ties become.

At the same time, the mother begins to sunder her connections with her young. Weaning is an important part of loosening the bonds. Gradually the mother grows less inclined to nurse her cubs. Eventually, instead of waiting for them expectantly, she begins to roll over, or even walks away, when they approach. They follow, nosing at her, sometimes becoming extremely pesky, but their persistence is likely to elicit only a snarl or growl from the mother.

All the while, the cubs are developing a new set of associations, those they will need as adults to perpetuate their kind. The young cats begin forming these new bonds as soon as they start playing with one another. Just as it helps prepare a cub for hunting, play serves as an introduction to the social behavior that a big cat needs to reach its full potential as an adult. When, for example, the young big cat tussles with its siblings in playful combat, it is also working out the fighting techniques it will need as an adult to defend its territory against rivals. Muscles and endurance are strengthened by seemingly endless hours of wrestling and chasing—activities that may look rough but are carried on with sheathed claws and sham bites.

Through play, the cub becomes familiar with others of its kind besides its mother, even though they may only be brothers and sisters. Romps with siblings promote identification of a cub with its species, which is basic to later breeding behavior.

The importance of play as a prelude to joining society as a full member can be seen most readily in the big cats that are truly social—the lion and to some extent the cheetah. The lion pride, particularly, lives by a set of rules shaped by ages of evolution. The rules ultimately promote the survival of the lions—not so much the individuals, or even the pride, but the species. The bonds that join the members of the pride into a cohesive unit are strong, as they must be to permit such large, aggressive animals to live together with a minimum of conflict. Through play, a lion cub develops the behavior that makes pride living possible.

One of the rules governing lion society is that each pride is headed by a dominant male, often with a few subordinate males as companions. Usually these males are not born in the pride, but come from elsewhere, after having left their own prides. Young males almost always part with their native prides at about three years of age. Departure comes after they are ignored or even harried by the lionesses and, if need be, driven away by the pride's leader.

The final breaking of bonds between parents and offspring of the other big cats takes various forms. The mother lynx or bobcat may simply stop paying attention to her young and walk away. A leopard or tiger family may break up gradually, as the growth of the cubs leads to a need to find more food. The cubs range ever farther afield in search of game, and finally disperse to establish their own hunting ranges. The romping, wrestling, and chasing of their early life have now been replaced by a new but related set of behavioral patterns, peculiar to the adults of their particular species.

157

Life Among the Wild Cats

night falls abruptly in the African savannah. In a sparse grove of yellow fever trees marking the banks of a small watercourse, the forms of waterbucks and zebras gathered there turn to inky shadows. Beyond, on the slightly rolling grassland, the immense herds of wildebeest assembled for seasonal migration are lost in the blackness. But their harsh, bawling calls and snorting are carried on the night air, testifying to their presence.

Moments pass, then a new sound begins, building in intensity until it overpowers all the other noises. It is the roaring of the lion pride. Somewhere out in the darkness, perhaps near a clump of thorn scrub or on one of the mounds of granitic rock that dot the plains, the members of the pride announce that they are on the prowl.

The roaring, if listened to closely, begins with a thunderous grunting that increases in volume and tempo until it seems to come from everywhere. It is probably the most awesome sound made by an animal, and it contributes mightily to the lion's reputation as the king of beasts. Roaring, loudest from the males, apparently has several functions, perhaps the most obvious being to warn possible trespassers that the pride has staked out the neighborhood as its own.

Maintaining its own piece of savannah is basic to the existence of the lion pride. Scientists have found that much more is involved in this than merely living in a particular territory and defending its borders. Observations of lion prides in the wild show that these groups are complex societies, especially when compared with the much more solitary patterns of the other big cats. Before considering the ways in which the other cats interact with members of their species, therefore, a close look at the life of the pride is in order.

Led by a dominant male who seems to be served by a retinue of lithe huntresses, the lion pride might look like the ultimate patriarchy. Appearances, in this case, are extremely deceptive. True, the females do most of the hunting, but the popular image of the male lion as a pampered potentate is far from accurate. The essence of the lion pride is the females and their young. Most females live their entire lives in the pride. Males never do. Often they belong for only a few months before they are killed or, for one reason or another, leave. The dominant male is but a transitory figure. At any time he may be challenged by a rival and deposed or killed. But as long as he is in power, the male must be ever ready to risk his life to preserve the integrity of the pride and its realm.

The size of a pride's range varies, depending on the abundance of game and the number of lions, which may be anywhere from three or four to three dozen.

Preceding pages:
Recent studies have revealed that cheetahs, long believed to be mostly solitary, do interact socially with one another. Left: Male lions battle for dominance over a pride. A pride leader may be deposed at any time. Some zoologists believe that the lion with the thicker mane has a better chance of winning because the mane protects the throat, the vital spot attacked by the rival.

It can cover an area of less than twenty square miles to more than five times that. Members of the pride may stay together or be scattered throughout the area, coming together in groups of a few each. Seasonally, the pride usually moves around the range in a fairly organized pattern. During the dry season, for example, it may move into a portion of its land that has permanent water, or into a wooded area, which is more likely to support game than the dusty savannah. With the coming of rain, the pride may return to the more arid country, suddenly verdant from the increased moisture. This is the extent to which the pride moves. Previously, scientists believed that lion prides were truly migratory, following the game herds on their long seasonal treks, but apparently this is not so. Even when migrations take the large herds out of a pride's realm, the lions remain.

Particularly where prides are numerous, or where their ranges are large, the boundaries of different holdings may overlap. This does not necessarily mean that both prides use the shared ground simultaneously. In most cases it is used only by one group at a time. Even the smallest ranges are large enough so that

161

Scientists do not fully understand why lions roar. Some think that roaring may express satisfaction or exuberance, while others feel that it may serve to warn other lions of territorial boundaries. It is now known that lions do not roar as an aid to hunting, as was once believed.

long periods pass during which a pride does not visit much of its realm.

Biologist George Schaller, observing prides on Tanzania's Serengeti Plain, discovered that the true stronghold of the pride is deep within its domain, and that there most of the group's activities take place. Lions from other prides seldom enter this part of the territory.

To the extent that such a description can be made, a typical lion pride has about fifteen members. The core of the pride is the adult females, perhaps a half-dozen or more. Two or three males, headed by the dominant lion, complete the adult population. The others are cubs and adolescents.

Almost always, all the females of the pride are related, perhaps spanning several generations. The adult males also may be kin, but not to the females, and rather than being of different generations are all about the same age. These differences between the males and females result from the continual shifting of dominant males.

The majority of usurpers who challenge and oust dominant males are outsiders, not pride cubs that have grown up and rebelled. A challenger usually is accompanied by one or two vassal males. Often these subordinate companions are siblings or cousins of the challenger, from the same pride. They grew up and left their natal pride together, and roamed in a group until they came on a new pride

The lion pride is a good example of an extended family, with the young and females of several generations living side by side, along with a few males. Although these cats play roughly with one another at mealtimes, the members of a pride generally get along well. Real disputes are rare, even when males are competing for females.

Lions usually lead a peaceful life. Prides are stable social units that may remain together for years. Females drive away strange females, and males do battle with male intruders. The lionesses generally stay together all their lives, but the males leave when they are about three and a half years old and wander until they are able to join a new pride.

166

Opposite: A male lion is reprimanded for biting his partner during mating. Lions may mate as often as twenty times a day during the female's estrus. If the female does not become pregnant, she will come into heat again in one to three months. When she is ready to give birth, the lioness seeks out a sheltered site away from the pride. She and her cubs rejoin the pride six weeks later. Left: A lioness nurses her litter.

ripe for the taking. The subordinates may even help their leader attack the head of the pride they seek to join. Of course, if the dominant male of the pride has a few vassals of his own, his chances of maintaining his leadership are much greater than if he were alone. For this reason, very few prides have only one adult male.

Battles between male lions are savage affairs, with clawing and biting that often leaves both antagonists ripped and tattered. Particularly when one lion is fighting against two or more, the loser may be so badly bitten he dies. Rarely, lions killed in such battles are eaten by their conquerors. The bigger a male's mane, the better chance he may have of surviving. Scientists believe that the thick, matted hair of the mane, which surrounds the vital areas of the neck, may be a natural armor against the fangs and claws of other lions. However, males with scrubby manes or no manes at all are not uncommon, and in some areas are even abundant. Whether the mane really is critical to survival, therefore, is questionable.

Once a dominant male, or even one of the subordinates, has been killed or driven away, a pride is extremely vulnerable. Other prides may chase it from its territory, or the usurping males may slaughter the cubs sired by the lions that

169

Lions sometimes sleep in the branches. In Tanzania's Lake Manyara National Park, lions frequently ascend even very tall trees. Ordinarily, however, lions stick to terrestrial pursuits. Their tawny coat blends remarkably well with the savannah grass.

were expelled.

The dominant male's protection of his pride does not extend to male cubs when they approach a size at which they can challenge him for overlordship. At this stage in their lives—when they are between two and three years old—the young males are harassed and repeatedly pursued by the adults, until they finally leave the pride, usually in a group. Once their links with the pride are severed, the young males become wanderers, traveling over vast stretches of the countryside, crossing the boundaries of many prides. Some rove areas of hundreds of square miles. Frequently, the lions that do not

belong to prides, and thus have no permanent territorial ties, follow the seasonal migrations of the game herds.

Although most of the wandering lions are males, some females are among them. Occasionally, for reasons not fully fathomed, young lionesses are chased from the pride, just as their male counterparts are. They are continually rebuffed by the other females, even sometimes by the males, until they begin to spend more and more time away from the pride and finally leave permanently.

The nomadic life is temporary for most lions, although they may wander for two years or longer before joining or ap-

propriating a pride. Furthermore, they may at any time be sent packing by another male and thus be forced to resume the unaffiliated life.

Even when not attached to a pride, lions exhibit their highly social instincts, for they seldom travel alone. Two, three, or more lions—sometimes all the same sex, sometimes mixed—may associate in groups. If they are large, these groups resemble prides at first glance, although they can in no way be considered as such, because they lack the pride's complex social organization. They are nothing more than loose assemblages, and most are rather temporary. Often they stay together only a few days.

Unlike the prides, which usually are hostile toward one another, lions that lack pride affiliations generally accept one another's company, although the first meeting, especially if it is over a kill, may be accompanied by a minor spat. A newcomer to a group may be swatted or chased for a short distance, but if it is persistent it eventually gains the tolerance of the others.

This is not at all the case when a strange, unaffiliated lion approaches a pride. The interloper is greeted with the same aggression displayed toward other prides. Aggressiveness, however, seems to be reserved for strangers of the same sex. A pride lion is not nearly as likely to attack a new lioness as he is to charge a strange male. Similarly, pride lionesses

Ocelots mating. Zoologists do not know for certain whether ocelots have a fixed breeding season or can reproduce at any time of year. Although they are the most common jungle cat in the Americas, ocelots are seldom seen by humans because they are primarily nocturnal and very shy.

are a bit more tolerant of male strangers, although when cubs are present the lionesses may band together to attack males that come too close. This behavior is not surprising, since strange males occasionally kill pride cubs.

Strangely, perhaps, the lionesses' intense reaction against a threatening male is not paralleled by direct concern for the endangered cubs. One lioness whose cubs were killed by strange males promptly sat down and ate one of her deceased offspring. In another case, an unaffiliated male that approached a pride over a kill was chased several times after he had bitten one of the group's cubs. Though they vigorously pursued the stranger, the lionesses paid no attention to the bleeding, squalling cub.

Be that as it may, studies of lion prides have shown repeatedly that the birth of cubs has a marked effect on the behavior of the pride. The pride as a whole becomes much more aggressive toward strangers. Within the pride, however, the effect is the opposite. The arrival of cubs promotes more harmonious relationships among the pride members, and the spirit of fellowship continues as long as the cubs are young.

Most lion cubs are born during seasonal dry periods—between June and October in eastern and southern Africa, during January and February in the Gir Forest of India. However, birth can occur at any time, because there is no particular season at which lionesses come into estrus, or heat.

Like the lion, the other big cats inhabiting the tropics can breed at any time of the year. New tiger cubs, for example, have been observed year-round in the tropical portion of their range, although sometimes the births are clustered at certain times of the year. A study conducted in India several decades ago, when tigers were more common, indicated that most cubs are born in November and April. However, young cubs have also been seen in June, March, May, and other months.

In the north, the mating of tigers and the arrival of the young are restricted to definite seasons. The tigers of northern Asia mate in midwinter, and the cubs arrive slightly more than three months later. The leopard, which has a gestation period similar to that of the tiger, follows the same pattern.

New World cats whose ranges span the tropics and the temperate zones have similar breeding patterns. Jaguars in northern Mexico mate in January or February and bear young about a hundred days later. Cougars in North America mate in late winter; their gestation period is about three months, so the young are born in the spring or early summer. Tropical jaguars and cougars can have their young at any time of year.

Having a fixed mating season is obviously an adaptation to living in tem-

The leopard's markings break up its body contours so that it blends into its leafy, sun-dappled surroundings in the forest. No two leopards have the same pattern of spots. The most athletic of the big cats, the leopard is excellent at running, jumping, tree-climbing, and swimming. It is usually a solitary hunter but will hunt with its mate during the breeding season.

175

perate regions, where the changing seasons bring sharp climatic differences. Mating in midwinter ensures that the young will be born in spring, when the weather is becoming milder and the young have a better chance of surviving. The species on which the cats prey also are bearing young in the spring, making food more abundant and easier to obtain.

Not surprisingly, cats that live solely in northern latitudes have very fixed breeding seasons. Lynxes and bobcats mate in February and March. Their gestation period is two months, which in their range places the birth of the young in the early spring. The snow leopard, which inhabits high mountains and thus lives in an arctic climate even where its range is close to the tropics, breeds as the alpine winter is ending. The cubs are born a little more than three months later, well after the weather has turned warmer and most of the snow has vanished.

During courtship and mating, the big cats seem to shed all their covertness and secrecy. To American pioneers, the cougar was known as the "screamer" because of the way it communicates its need to mate. Sometimes audible a mile away, the call usually is described as resembling a woman's scream conveying extreme terror.

There have been reports of several male tigers fighting at once over a mate, but scientists believe that courtship combats between these cats seldom cause se-

rious injuries. Lions within a pride fight even less over the lionesses, but perhaps that is to be expected from such a social animal. Their conflicts are limited to occasional swats, snarls, and rare momentary wrestling that may result in a cut or two, but little more.

All the adult males in a pride have a chance to mate with the lionesses, frequently even with the same one. When a lioness is in heat, she may be courted by each of the males in the pride. A male indicates his interest by closely following the female about. Sometimes she may grow extremely playful, leading the male on feverish chases, waiting for him, then rebuffing him with a snarl. The male stays close, sniffing and licking the lioness, sometimes rubbing noses with her. If she accepts him, they mate, accompanied by some yowling, although not nearly so much as in some other cats. Once paired off, lions may mate repeatedly, sometimes ten or twenty times a day.

As more solitary animals, tigers court and mate in a manner different from that of the lions, but generally typical of the other big cats. Each tiger, male or female, has a special home range. Tigers with ranges near one another come into contact, and if the female is in heat, may mate. Thus, while tigers are in no way monogamous—as, scientists have found, jaguars are—the same pair may mate repeatedly and have several sets of offspring over a period of years.

178

When hunting, cheetahs find strength in numbers. A lone cheetah can bring down only small prey, such as gazelles, but a group can pursue game as large as zebras and wildebeests. Groups may consist of all males, or mostly males with a few females, but never of females only. After mating, a male and female remain together for a long time, with the male helping to raise the young.

When a tigress is in heat, she roars and makes loud, moaning sounds to attract a mate. Males answer when they hear her call. The tigress in heat is very restless, frequently moving about fitfully, rolling on her back, and making sounds resembling loud snorts.

Once a male and female have found one another, they may begin to brush up against one another and touch with their forepaws. Eventually, if all goes well, they mate. Tigers are extremely noisy during intercourse. They emit thunderous roars and periodic loud grunts and snarls. The tiger pair may remain together and continue to mate on and off for the duration of the female's estrus, perhaps as long as two weeks. After that, until the cubs are born, the two may associate for short periods, although the meetings are probably accidental.

The degree to which tigers are sociable has been a matter of some contention among scientists who have studied these cats. No one has suggested that tigers are not solitary hunters, but some observers say that at times several of them, outside of the family group or mating pair, get along quite well together.

During the nineteenth and early twentieth centuries, when tigers were more abundant, hunters and naturalists reported seeing groups of tigers numbering a half-dozen or more. The attraction that seems to draw tigers together is game, particularly a kill. Some scientists

180

say that groups of tigers observed by researchers in the field were gathered unnaturally, lured by the presence of bait. (When studying wild tigers, scientists commonly stake out a cow or domestic buffalo to attract the cats and bring them within observing range.) But researchers who ascribe some degree of sociability to tigers say that when living is easy for tigers, temporary groups are likely to form. This may explain the reports of groups from past years, before so much of the tiger's habitat and game were destroyed, and before the cats themselves were scarce.

Groups of tigers have been observed several times over baits by Dr.

Charles McDougal, director of operations at the Tiger Tops Jungle Lodge in the Royal Chitawan National Park of Nepal. Tigers in small groups at baits do not engage in mass gorging as lions do, but instead feed individually. After one tiger has finished eating, it moves away from the carcass while the next one begins to feed. Observations made by students of tiger behavior over many years indicate that the only times that more than one tiger will feed simultaneously and harmoniously on the same prey is when the victim is very large—an elephant, for example. In such cases, tigers feed on different parts of the carcass and thus re-

Despite their reputation as nearly invincible predators, tigers must work hard to make a living. They often wait at waterholes where prey animals gather, but even when game is abundant they may go several days without a kill.

main apart. Simultaneous feeding by tigers, however, is extremely unusual.

When gathered around a victim but not feeding, tigers may sit or lie a few yards apart. Sometimes they may rub against one another very briefly, or even make tentative attempts to play. Mostly, though, they keep a seemingly respectful distance from one another, with little or no tension between them.

The concept of the cheetah as a solitary creature also has undergone some revision in recent years, as a result of observations in zoos as well as field studies. Except for a few efforts in the 1950s, zoos were unable to breed cheetahs with any

real success until the late 1960s, when it was recognized that these cats reproduce best when a female is kept with more than one male. This observation conforms with those of cheetahs in the wild. Because cheetahs often spread out over very wide areas they were, until a decade or two ago, thought to be extremely solitary, unsociable creatures. This is far from the truth, for cheetahs do indeed spend much of their time together, more so than tigers but less than lions. Almost always, there are more males than females in a group of cheetahs, and a female in heat may mate with several males.

Groups of cheetahs may range in

183

size from a handful or animals to several dozen. Some of these groups are small family units, composed of a mother and her young cubs. Others are composed exclusively of adults. A theory suggested by some scientists is that the cheetah's basic social unit is a band of males on the lookout for females that will join them to mate. This hypothesis is based on the fact that while groups of mixed sexes and all males are common, troops composed entirely of females are almost never seen. Also suggested is the possibility that the adult groups are organized along family lines, perhaps young cheetahs that have matured and remained together. A study of cheetahs made in Kenya in the 1960s revealed no interchange of individuals between groups, which could support the grown-family theory.

It is possible that adult cheetah groups assemble at definite locations. Unlike lion prides, they do not seem to have their own private kingdoms. Instead, several groups may wander through the same expanse of grassland, although they refrain from contact with one another. One area observed over two days was used by thirteen different groups.

Whether all masculine or of both sexes, groups of adult cheetahs always appear to be led by a male, no matter what the size of the group. A pair of males watched in one study, for example, was obviously composed of a leader and follower. One always walked ahead of the

Opposite: When they are eating, tigers may drink large quantities of water. Often a tiger will lug the carcass of a large victim a considerable distance to reach the water before it begins to eat. Left: A tiger cleans itself after a meal.

other. If the "follower" attempted to deviate from the course, the lead male paid no heed and continued on his way until the other returned and fell in line.

For a long time, it was assumed that cheetahs were purely solitary hunters. The results of recent studies, however, indicate that they sometimes may pursue prey as a group, although certainly with nothing like the coordinated tactics of the lion pride. In some cases the male leader seems to initiate the group attack. For instance, two male cheetahs and a female were observed lazing during the heat of the day, when some wart hogs, nibbling at the low shoots of savannah grass, approached within striking distance. One of the males—the subordinate,

185

Opposite: Tigers, well camouflaged in the forest, remain hidden in cover until they are close enough to rush their prey. Left: Although usually solitary, male and female tigers sometimes join one another to hunt during the breeding season. Both sexes mark their territories by urinating and scratching trees.

as it turned out—started to walk toward the wild pigs, as did the female. But the leader continued to rest, and the other two cheetahs turned away from the wart hogs and came back to him. A short time later, the leader apparently decided that the time was ripe for the hunt. This time he led and the other two followed.

While small gazelles such as the Thompson's are the cheetah's main prey on the African savannahs, the swift cats sometimes take larger animals. Zebras and big antelopes such as topi and wildebeest are occasionally preyed on by cheetahs, but usually only when the cats hunt together. A lone cheetah is hard-pressed to bring down such big animals. Group living, therefore, may be important for hunting as well as for reproduction.

Much remains to be learned about the organization of cheetah groups and their function in terms of evolutionary survival. The nature and size of groups may differ according to geography and environmental conditions, although this has not been proven. Studies of the associations of cheetahs have provided varying evidence. Some showed that most cheetahs in a given area were solitary, and that groups of more than two animals were relatively uncommon. Others indicated that most of the animals were in groups, often of more than two. Despite the unsettled questions, the old image of the cheetah as a loner has been dispelled.

In contrast to the total or at least partial sociability of the lion, cheetah, and tiger are the life styles of the other 187

big cats, which are completely solitary except during the breeding season. Leopards, lynxes, snow leopards, and the rest lead lives of astonishing independence, avoiding others of their kind with extreme determination. If contact is made, even between male and female (again, outside of the breeding season), it is only because one has ventured into the other's area. Such situations are tense and may occasionally lead to fighting, depending on how territorial the species involved is.

The territoriality of animals is a concept that has been discussed interminably in both popular and scientific literature, yet "territoriality" remains an ill-defined term. It may mean a variety of things to behaviorists and field biologists, the scientists most concerned with it.

The word "territory" is sometimes used loosely to describe the entire area used by an animal—the land in which it hunts, mates, sleeps, eats, and so on. On the other hand, a territory is sometimes considered to be only the relatively small portion of the land habitually used by an animal. This special piece of countryside may be just a few square yards for a small creature, or several square miles for some big cats. Very often this restricted "territory" is vigorously defended by the animal, sometimes to the death. In this context, the inner domain of the area inhabited by a lion pride—described earlier as its "stronghold"—is its territory. The rest of the area is its "home range."

For some big cats, perhaps, home range and territory are synonymous. In

Opposite: A tiger standing in the rain may look uncomfortable, but this great striped cat is not at all averse to water. Tigers can even withstand cold precipitation such as sleet and snow. Left: Males generally defend the heart of their territory against others of their own sex.

the opinion of certain researchers, the home range of a tiger, sometimes more than a hundred square miles, coincides with its territory, but this is true only for the males. Several females may have home ranges that overlap parts of a male's territory, though they seldom overlap each other's. In effect, according to this way of thinking, the male maintains a personal realm, parts of which are used by different females that, when in heat, are available for mating. The boundaries of the males' ranges keep them apart but are by no means rigid. Borders change as males die or leave and others arrive.

There is some evidence that the tiger's territory may not always extend to the limits of its home range. Like lions unaffiliated with prides, some male tigers lack specific pieces of land as territories and wander the countryside. These animals seem to have free passage through the lands of the territorial males. Moreover, it appears that some tigers focus their activities on particular parts of their range, rather in the manner of lions. It may be that a tiger can have several of these areas within its total range, and that wanderers are tolerated elsewhere. According to another view, the home ranges of even male tigers may overlap, but because they are so large two tigers are seldom in a sensitive area at once. It would follow, therefore, that tigers may be spaced not only by distance but by time.

Another aspect of territoriality that has aroused the curiosity of scientists is revealed by a study of lions inhab-

189

iting Nairobi National Park, which abuts the industries and homes four miles from the center of Kenya's capital. The park's 44 square miles of rolling savannah were divided by approximately two dozen resident lions into four pride home ranges. The ranges were relatively small in comparison with those in other areas, and their boundaries were frequently crossed by all of the prides. Lions from one pride often penetrated deep into the range of another group. The landholding lions, however, did not go out of their way to stay on the lookout for the intruders. In fact, they did not even patrol their range to keep the others out. If the intruders happened to come across the landholders, however, the latter acted as if they were defending territory. This situation could mean that the lions had a "floating" territory. In other words, wherever the pride went in its home range, a certain amount of space surrounding it was considered inviolable. The location of the territory corresponded to the location of the pride.

The idea of a floating territory has been applied to tigers by some behaviorists. If it is correct, then the personal territory of a tiger probably expands and contracts as the situation warrants. During the mating season, perhaps, the male tiger insists that other males give him plenty of room. At harmonious gatherings of tigers such as those described earlier, however, the personal territories shrink to only a few square yards at most.

Male and female jaguars stay together only during the breeding season. The female bears two to four cubs, which remain with her for two years. Jaguars hunt within specific territories, which vary in size depending on the amount of game available.

191

Snarling its defiance, a bobcat is a tough adversary for dogs and other enemies. The bobcat is a highly adaptable and extremely secretive animal. Depending on the region in which they live, bobcats may differ slightly from one another in the color and texture of their coats, but all belong to the same species.

For the big cats, territoriality may be strongly influenced by the availability of food. When food is scarce, for example, bobcats expand their ranges from a few square miles to dozens. Instead of keeping to a small, local hunting area, a lynx faced with a shortage of hares may range far afield, sometimes hundreds of miles. Similar extension of range has been documented for jaguars.

The only thing scientists can say with any certainty is that the territoriality of the big cats is highly variable, even within the same species. One study of leopards on the African savannah found that individuals had ranges from about ten square miles to more than 160 square miles. Another study, in Sri Lanka, put the home range of leopards on part of that island at only a few square miles. Ranges of leopards on the Serengeti Plain overlapped, according to one researcher's observations. In Sri Lanka, where the ranges were very small, boundaries were much more distinct.

Disparity exists in the way big cats defend their holdings. The leopard provides a good example of how such behavior can vary even within a species. At least two scientists who have studied leopards in Africa say that there was little evidence of the animals actively defending any sort of range or territory. In India, however, the situation may be different, for there territorial combat between leopards has been witnessed.

As a rule, though, leopards seem to shun one another scrupulously. So do cougars—which, in winter, at least, have a home-range system resembling the one suggested for the tiger. The dominions of male cougars may extend more than thirty square miles and overlap the ranges of females, but not those of other males. There are wanderers among the cougars, too, which move freely across boundaries. Cougars tolerate the presence of strangers traveling through, but both the holder of a territory and the newcomer take pains to avoid meeting. Such behavior prevents the possibility of dangerous combat, which is reserved for the mating season.

While lions, and less commonly tigers, may fight ferociously to drive out intruders, often it is not necessary. As with other animals, the big cat standing on its own ground has an edge over the stranger. A wandering tiger in the home range of another may even leave its kill simply because the one that occupies the area is approaching. Two incidents involving lions are very much to the point here. In one, two lionesses and a young male had killed a wart hog on land held by a pride. Though none of the pride members was visible, the trio nevertheless left the carcass for several minutes while they explored the neighborhood. Only after it was obvious that the pride was not in the area did the three lions return and begin to eat. The other incident concerns a large male that had pen-

etrated far into a pride's home range. When the pride males began roaring a mile away, he immediately scooted for home.

Calls are an important signaling device for other cats besides lions. Certainly the bobcat's screeches serve to mark territory. Tigers seem to roar to alert others to their presence, but not nearly as frequently as lions. Leopards utter loud, rasping cries while patrolling their ranges. Jaguars emit short, grunting roars while making their rounds.

Vocalizations are just one of the ways in which the big cats proclaim their rights to a piece of land without entering direct combat. By advertising their presence, the big cats can effectively keep others off their grounds without resorting to force and thus risking death. Such means of avoiding combat are adaptations that promote the survival of the cats.

Cats often spray urine and scrape the ground or a tree trunk to mark their territories. The urine is mixed with glandular secretions that intensify the scent. The cougar scrapes up a mass of twigs, leaves, and other vegetation, heaps it into a low mound, and urinates on it. The lion sprays either on a bush or on the ground. If a bush is the target, the cat first rubs its head against the leaves. Then it sprays backward. Lions also may rake the ground with their hind claws, then urinate on the torn-up soil. Lynxes scratch tree trunks and use their feces as markers. Cheetahs urinate on the grass, and if there are trees

The lynx (opposite top and left) is a close cousin of the bobcat (opposite bottom). The bobcat is sometimes called the bay lynx. Lynxes, which live in North America, Europe, and Asia, generally inhabit more northern areas than bobcats, which are found only in North America.

around, they scratch the bark. One group of cheetahs was seen scratching the same tree day after day as they passed it on tours of their range. Leopards scrape trees as well as the ground, and they urinate both on their scrapes and on vegetation. They even mark branches with their urine. Tigers mark much the way lions do, and they also deposit feces as markings.

More often than not, it is the male cats that do the marking, but female leopards and tigers do it, too. The accuracy with which a tigress can aim her urine was vividly demonstrated to a newspaper photographer who was taking a picture of a mother and cubs at the Bronx Zoo. Standing a few yards away, the tigress turned her tail toward the newsman, lifted it, and directed a stream that thoroughly drenched the surprised man.

A bobcat taking its ease in a small stream shows that, like some of its larger relatives, it has a liking for water. Though the bobcat preys mostly on birds and small mammals, it sometimes goes into the water to catch aquatic creatures.

Cats scratch, scrape, urinate, and call as they patrol their territories, often on routes that are taken day after day (or night after night, as the case may be). Just as cheetahs scratch at the same trees repeatedly, cougars have definite marking stations, and lions often urinate on the same bushes. The pattern holds for most of the cats.

Even a big cat's posture can be a signal to others that it is standing on its home ground. As perhaps befits the creature people call the king of beasts, the male lion provides the best example. Sometimes, to demarcate his realm, he stands tall and erect, parading about the most conspicuous sites, so there is no mistake about who occupies the land.

The two white spots behind the ears of a tiger also may serve a purpose in marking territory. Unlike the tiger's stripes, which blend into the shadows of the brush and forest, the prominent spots behind the ears make the cat more visible when its ears are raised. The tiger's body may be completely camouflaged as it lies low, but once it lifts its ears the spots stand out vividly and can be seen from a long distance, at least a hundred yards. This is true even if the tiger is moving through cover. During his classic study of tigers in India's Kanha National Park, George Schaller was twice alerted to the presence of hidden tigers by their ear spots. The spots are especially visible when the tiger grimaces in anger, for then the ears are erect and turned forward. Scientists have suggested that by showing the spots, the tiger indicates its readiness to attack. Schaller has theorized that the spots may also help one tiger follow another—a cub its mother, for instance—in dense foliage. It is not unreasonable to suspect that if the spots help tigers see one another, the markings may well be used to register territorial claims. If people can see the ear spots from a distance, there is little doubt that other tigers can, too. The spots may enable a tiger to assert its territorial rights merely by raising its ears and turning them back and forth, without exposing the rest of its body.

Whether a cat socializes or travels its home area alone, it still is part of a larger feline society, and it relates to others of its species in predictable ways. The very act of avoidance practiced by a cougar or leopard, for example, is a form of social interaction. So, certainly, is marking, or roaring to ward off intruders from a distance.

Up close, the big cats use a surprisingly varied number of vocalizations to communicate. Tigers coming together for a friendly meeting puff air through their nostrils and lips to make a gentle snoring sound. Scientists have given it the technical name *prusten*, but perhaps "chuffling" is more descriptive, because that is exactly what it sounds like.

Chuffling is a sign of affection among tigers and seems to be especially important when tigers approach one another. Zoo tigers often chuffle when they approach familiar people. A large tiger at the Bronx Zoo, on seeing its favorite cu-rator, would lower its head and amble to the edge of its enclosure, chuffling all the while. The cat even would respond this way to a new acquaintance if the person learned to chuffle with moderate skill.

The tiger's hissing snarls convey something quite different—growing anger. Eventually, if the situation worsens, the snarls are followed by a coughing roar, generally produced as the tiger charges. Bobcats have a similar repertoire, ranging from spitting and hisses when alarmed to a sudden, explosive cough when very angry. The cheetah, not a particularly noisy cat, yelps loudly when threatened. Within a group, whether a mother and young or all adults, cheetahs communicate by emitting sounds best described as "chirps." The young cubs of most big cats mew to attract parental attention. The adults usually answer by grunting.

As anyone who has watched a house cat knows, felines can make their feelings known quite graphically with facial expressions and posturing. Most of the expressions and postures are common to all cats and have similar meanings. Bared fangs, for instance, signify anger or a response to threat. When cats greet, they rub heads. At its ease, a cat has a totally relaxed expression, ears erect but not tense, lips closed but not tightly, and eyes slightly droopy. Possibly no other face in the animal kingdom says so well that at that moment, all is right with the world.

The Smaller Kin

the sinuous grace and power of the big cats are reflected in a host of other wild felines that inhabit Africa, the Americas, and Eurasia. Most of these creatures are smaller than the species already described, although a few approach the size of the lesser big cats. One of the smaller cats, the strange species inhabiting Japan's Iriomote Island, was mentioned in Chapter 1 as a possible model of the ancestral felines of prehistoric times. The mystery that surrounds the Iriomote cat typifies the lack of knowledge about many of the smaller cats, which are, if anything, more secretive than their larger relatives. Some of the small wild cats, though they have been known to science for generations, have been observed even less than the Iriomote cat, which was discovered only a few years ago. This is especially true of the cats that inhabit deep jungles, such as those of the Amazon basin and Southeast Asia.

Similar in color to the ocelot, and with roughly the same range—from the South American tropics north to the fringes of the United States border—the margay (*Felis wiedi*) is smaller, weighing less than 20 pounds. Like the ocelot, it is an adept climber and seems especially suited to the forest, but it also adapts to scrubby desert and mesquite country. Small birds, rats, and similar creatures probably supply the margay with most of its food. It is also known to feast on frogs, lizards, and even insects. Exactly how it hunts is not really known, for while it is often kept in captivity, the extremely secretive margay has almost never been observed in the wild. The margay is as skillful a climber as the larger clouded leopard of Southeast Asia, and where it inhabits forests it almost certainly can catch prey in the trees. It has wide, flexible feet with which it can hang from branches. Perhaps only a few other mammals—some of the monkeys, and possibly some squirrels—are as at home in the trees as the margay.

The margay rarely makes it into the United States, and when it does it only gets into an extremely small area just north of the Rio Grande, northeast of Brownsville, Texas.

About the same size as the margay is another tropical cat with a range that just barely includes part of the United States. This is the jaguarundi (*Felis yagouaroundi*), also known as the eyra. The jaguarundi lives as far south as Paraguay and as far north as the United States border. Farther east, jaguarundis have been turning up in various locations in Florida for the past several years. These cats did not reach Florida naturally; they are apparently either escaped or abandoned pets. They seem to be surviving in their new habitat, and very likely they are breeding in some parts of the state.

A rather unusual cat, the jaguarundi departs somewhat in appearance from the ordinary feline form, and has

traits that make it look almost weasel-like. In Mexico, in fact, the jaguarundi is known as the "otter cat." Its body, including its head, is long and low, and its ears are relatively smaller than those of other cats. It also resembles the curious fossa of Madagascar, a creature once believed to be feline but now grouped with the mongooses and civets.

While many cats have color phases—as, for example, the black jaguar or leopard—few have as many varieties as the jaguarundi. Some are reddish-brown, others are dark gray, while still others may be bluish-black. Between these extremes is an array of other shades. Unlike the color phases of other cats, those of the jaguarundi are spread fairly evenly through the population, although the very black individuals are less common than the other types. For a long time, scientists believed that there were two separate species of jaguarundi, one grayish and the other with a reddish coat. The different colors, however, can appear within a single litter.

Jaguarundis have a gestation period of a little more than two months, after which two spotted young usually are born. The spots fade with age. There is

201

debate over when the main reproductive seasons occur, although observers have reported that in the northern portions of its range, the jaguarundi mates mostly in late autumn and early winter.

Jaguarundis prefer heavy brush, like the scrubby oaks of the chaparral that grows on low mountain slopes in arid areas of northern Mexico, and the edges of jungles, where rainfall is abundant. An excellent swimmer and not loath to plunge into the water, this cat also inhabits swamps.

From the low, slim shape of the jaguarundi's body, it is evident that the cat spends most of its time on the ground, slipping under and through the brush, rather than climbing among the branches.

The jaguarundi pictured at left was photographed in southern Arizona, near the northernmost limits of its range. The jaguarundi shown below is from tropical South America, the heart of the cat's range. Though the jaguarundi is able to climb, it spends most of its time on the ground.

If chased by dogs, however, it will ascend the nearest tall tree and try to hide. The jaguarundi hunts a variety of ground-dwelling animals, including quail, rabbits, and rodents, especially mice, wood rats, and cotton rats. Around water it will eat frogs.

In the northern portions of its range, where there is plenty of low brush to conceal it, the jaguarundi hunts during the day. Farther south, it inhabits tropical forests, where there are few thickets. Contrary to the popular image of the tropical forest, or "jungle," there are few tangles of vegetation near the ground, because the forest canopy keeps out the sunlight. The only places in the jungle where low vegetation is thick are within clearings and near river banks, where the canopy is broken and the sun's rays penetrate to the earth. In jungles, the jaguarundi seeks the concealment of the night for hunting.

No larger than a hefty house cat is another feline of the American tropics, the little spotted cat (*Felis tigrina*). Yellow, with a variety of spots—rosettes near the rump, solid on the sides—this creature shuns open areas and clings to heavy jungle. Not much more is known about it than that it hunts small creatures such as birds and rodents, and that it spends much of its time in the trees. Observations of zoo captives have revealed that the gestation period is more than ten weeks long. The little spotted cat ranges from Central America to the northern Amazon basin.

The open country of South America, from Argentina north to Ecuador and Brazil, is the home of the pampas cat (*Felis colocolo*). About the size of a domestic cat, the pampas cat is a handsome animal, with long, rough, silvery gray fur and a harness of thin, dark stripes running over its back and all along its body. Over its eyes are two dark vertical bars that flare upward, giving the cat an unusually elegant look. A number of subspecies of the pampas cat, some inhabiting sparse forest and uplands as well as plains, also inhabit South America, hunting small mammals and birds on the ground.

The landscape after which the pampas cat is named is one of broad horizons, stretching from east-central Argentina west to the Andes and north to Bolivia and Paraguay, where it merges with open, scrubby savannah. The pampas are virtually treeless, dotted with broad marshes and flood plains that become immense, shallow lakes during the wet season. Because this area has very rich soil, it is prime agricultural land, and much of the pampas has been turned into grain fields and pasture. The change in the environment has reduced wildlife populations, and the pampas cat, never well known, has become increasingly rare and is now vanishing from much of its former range.

Several other small cats live in

As its name indicates, the pampas cat is native to the open plains of southern South America. It has thin, dark stripes in a pattern that resembles that of the domestic tabby cat. The pampas cat's fur is long and silvery.

205

South America. Among the most mysterious of all felines, they are seldom seen in the wild. It is not certain whether all belong to different species, or whether they are geographical variations of just a few species. Among these creatures is *Felis guigna* (it has no common English name), which roams the lower slopes of the Andes. It is a forest animal and a good climber, with coloration similar to the pampas cat's. Another is Geoffroy's cat (*Felis geoffroyi*), a graceful creature with a yellow background color and dark spots that become narrow stripes on the light-colored cheeks and neck.

Ranging from southern Brazil to Argentina, Geoffroy's cat likes low forest. It also wanders into the mountains. A good climber, it spends quite a lot of time resting on low branches, if its behavior in zoos is any indication of the way it acts in the wild. Many zoos keep Geoffroy's cats, but none has been very successful at breeding these South American felines. A geographical race, or subspecies, of this animal, the salt desert cat, roams the arid wastes of western Argentina, near the foothills of the Andes. Until the 1950s, it was thought to be an entirely different species, but it is now grouped with Geoffroy's cat.

About the size of Geoffroy's cat is another species, *Felis jacobita*, which roams the rocky slopes and cliffs of the Andes up to more than 16,000 feet. Gray with brown patches, this cat hunts largely above the timber line, where it preys on colonies of mountain viscachas and chinchillas, related rodents that are typical of the region. A mysterious animal, it goes about its life on the chill, bleak heights largely undetected by man.

The situation is quite different with Europe's only small cat. The wildcat (*Felis silvestris*), with an original range from the British Isles to Asia Minor, has been studied and commented on since ancient times. It closely resembles a domestic tabby, though it is slightly larger, with a broader head and a tail that does not taper. It has a gray to buff ground color and dark, often indistinct, vertical stripes descending from the ridge of the back. A woodland creature, the wildcat once was found in virtually every forested area from southern Scandinavia to the Mediterranean islands.

On the islands, and in southern Europe, a favorite haunt of the wildcat is the thick, almost impenetrable scrub known as *maquis* or *macchia*. Composed of various scrubby evergreen oaks, stunted pines, brambles, and other vegetation that can live in a relatively arid environment, the *macchia* covers the lower slopes of many mountains. Though highly susceptible to fire, *macchia* is able to keep a foothold on slopes that have been badly eroded, as is the case in the Mediterranean countries. At one time the lands rimming the Mediterranean were covered with mature forests, but these were cut

Extremely rare, the rusty-spotted cat is a native of India and Sri Lanka. It is about the same size as the domestic cat and prowls both forests and scrubby plains.

207

down long ago. Intensive use of the land, especially overgrazing by domestic stock, has caused devastating erosion. The *macchia* has invaded and covered slopes that were denuded of their forests and stripped of topsoil. Therefore, while not as attractive as a tall, green, forest, the scrubby *macchia* woodland has helped to preserve wildlife in an otherwise environmentally impoverished region.

Hundreds of years ago, the wildcat's numbers began to decline, especially in the northern areas of its range. As long ago as the sixteenth century, it was sought by bounty hunters in Great Britain. Records show that there was a price on the cat's head until the 1800s, when it disappeared from its last havens south of Scotland. The wildcat was last seen in England in the early 1840s, though it survived in Wales until near the end of the century.

Today the only place the animal can be found in the British Isles is in the highlands of Scotland, particularly in the Grampian Mountains. These mountains arc across the center of Scotland south of Loch Ness, ranging east from the county of Argyll to Aberdeen and Kincardine. They are covered both with scattered woodlands and with great moors, which extend to altitudes of more than 3,000 feet. The moors can be forbidding, especially at the higher altitudes, where the climate is cold and the terrain is swept by winds. Even domestic sheep are scarce on the highest moorlands. The moors do, however, support large herds of the great Scottish red deer, and they abound in grouse and rodents, prey of the wildcat. These creatures wander through the heath and heather that typify this largely treeless landscape. Landowners and farmers have come to realize that although the wildcat occasionally kills fawns and game birds, it also helps keep down the populations of rabbits and small rodents. Efforts are now being made to protect the species in Scotland.

Elsewhere, the wildcat has undergone a similar decline. Among its refuges in central Europe are the forests of the Ardennes and southern Germany. The cat is most common, however, in the rugged mountains of the Mediterranean countries from Spain to Turkey, and in the mountains of eastern Europe. Wildcats still rove the hills of Sicily and the *macchia* of Corsica and Sardinia. On these two islands, as well as in Asia Minor, the

The European wildcat is reputed to be extremely ferocious. While this cat is certainly fierce when aroused, it is no more feisty than most other small wild felines. When cornered, defending a kill, or protecting young, small cats will tackle animals much larger than they.

209

wildcat has differentiated into several fairly distinct subspecies. Some zoologists have suggested that these subspecies are actually intermediate forms between the European cat and the wildcats of Africa and Asia.

Wildcats are solitary, with a reputation for extreme savagery. The female wildcat is said to be especially ferocious when defending her young. Actually, the wildcat is neither more nor less fierce than any other small wild feline and, as some zoologists have observed, is no more savage than a domestic cat that has taken up life in the wild.

The wildcat hunts with superb stealth and speed. It often stalks birds and small mammals in thick, low vegetation, which provides the cover necessary to conceal the cat as it hugs the ground. It stays low until it creeps within range, freezing completely if the prey seems aware of impending danger. When it is close enough, the cat charges with a series of dazzling leaps that bring it down on its target in an instant. The prey of the wildcat comprises an incredible variety of animals, including young wild boars, fawns of the roe deer, rabbits, hares, grouse, pheasants, various rats and mice, songbirds, fish, and a number of domestic animals.

Very similar to the European wildcat is the African species, *Felis libyca,* occasionally referred to as the caffer cat. It inhabits almost all of Africa except the Sahara Desert and the wet equatorial forests of the central and western portions of the continent. It is also found in Arabia. Because it is nearly identical in size and appearance to the European species, some zoologists consider the two cats to be variants of the same species, but this is not a view that is shared by most scientists.

Shunning thick forest but thriving in scrub, bush, and savannah, the African wildcat also prowls the alleys of big cities within its range, where it readily interbreeds with domestic cats. Hybrids of domestic and wildcat parents abound around many of Africa's larger communities; in some cases hybridization has almost eliminated local populations of the wild species. While the general color and conformation of the hybrids is similar to that of the wildcat—both look like tabbies—there are some distinguishing differences. The wildcat has reddish fur behind its ears, a marking the hybrids lack. Moreover, the wildcat has longer legs than either the domestic type or the hybrids.

Interbreeding between the wildcat and domestic stock is not surprising, for the two are closely related. The wildcat, in fact, probably gave rise to most domestic breeds. Although small wildcats from several parts of Europe and Asia may have added their bloodlines to the different breeds of house cat, the main strain seems to have come from the African

The sand cat (adult above and young below) is an exceptionally attractive little feline. This cat inhabits deserts from North Africa and Arabia to Turkestan. Like many other small desert predators, it has large ears— an adaptation that seems to indicate its strong dependence on hearing to locate and catch prey.

211

212

animal.

Though there are scores of different breeds of domestic cats in the world, all belong to the same species, *Felis catus.* The domestic breed closest to the African and European wildcats is the tabby. This is the most common type of domestic cat, familiar to almost everyone. Its color may be anything from all white or all black to a mottled or tortoiseshell pattern. Many tabbies are conspicuously striped, with the stripes generally forming a yoke across the back and shoulders and running backward from the eyes and nose. The tabby's tail is narrow, its fur is short, and its ears are short and pointed.

Despite the tabby's closeness to the basic cat stock, most cat fanciers think of it as rather plain. Some of the other breeds, especially those that developed in Asia, are considerably more exotic. Among these are the Siamese and the long-haired Angoras and Persians. The Siamese cat seems to have come originally from China rather than from Siam (now Thailand). However, early in the nineteenth century, the royal house of Siam managed to obtain virtually all the Siamese cats available. Siamese cats did not find their way to the western world until near the turn of the century, when they were presented as gifts to westerners by Siamese royalty.

Domestic cats have turned feral—that is, reverted to the wild state—in many parts of the world, including areas that never had native cat populations. Feral cats are the scourge of game birds and other small wild animals. In the United States, feral cats are a much more serious threat to birds than most wild predators. Feral cats may have helped push some wild creatures toward extinction, especially in places where cats do not occur naturally. Cats have definitely played a part in reducing the populations of one of the most unusual reptiles in the world, the tuatara. This archaic, lizard-like creature survives only on a handful of rocky islets off New Zealand. It is the last survivor of a group of primitive reptiles known as "beak heads," which flourished during the time of the dinosaurs.

Top: Lurking in the grass of a park in South Africa, an African wildcat strikes a pose reminiscent of some of its larger kin. Bottom: An African wildcat at rest. This cat inhabits much of Africa, both countryside and cities, and is probably the main ancestor of the domestic cat.

213

Cats introduced by man on the tuatara's islands have become feral and now prey on the reptiles.

Cats were first domesticated about five thousand years ago, probably in Egypt. The Egyptians had a special reverence for felines. Their goddess of joy and love, Bastet, was depicted as a cat. Archeologists have discovered the remains of thousands of mummified pet cats. Egyptian cat owners often placed the mummies of their pets in elaborate cases, even in small tombs stocked with saucers of food for the cat to eat in the afterworld. Most of the mummies seem to be of African wildcats. The cats depicted in Egyptian art also have the long legs characteristic of the wildcat. Often these cats are shown in the act of hunting, going after small mammals and, in at least one artifact, snakes.

Snakes and lizards, in addition to birds and mammals, make up a good part of the wildcat's natural diet. Even invertebrates such as spiders and centipedes are eaten. The largest animal known to have been killed by an African wildcat is the springhaas, or springhare, a nine-pound rodent that resembles a giant kangaroo rat. Because it is such an avid hunter of rodents, the wildcat is one of the few African predators whose lot has been improved by increasing agriculturization of the savannah. Farms, with their fields of grain and other produce, support large populations of rats, mice, and other ro-

Considered by many to be the daintiest of cats, the little black-footed cat of southern Africa often inhabits old termite mounds. It shares the southern range of the African wildcat, and sometimes the two animals are confused. The large dark spots distinguish the black-footed cat.

dents, making hunting easier for the cats.

African wildcats are primarily nocturnal. During the day they hide in the bush or in rocky areas. Thickets and small caves also shelter the young of the wildcat, which usually produces litters of between two and five kittens. The cat breeds at any time of year.

A little smaller than the African wildcat is the sand cat (*Felis margarita*). A most unusual creature, this cat lives in scattered locations throughout the deserts of North Africa and Arabia, and in the rocky wastelands of the Soviet Union east of the Caspian Sea (the area formerly known as Turkestan). Its basic body color is the same as the sand in which it lives. The long, gray hair covering its soles protects it against the heat of the sand and provides support, just as the hairy feet of the snow leopard provide insulation against the cold and support in the snow. The sand cat seems to live on desert rodents and birds. Like many other desert animals, sand cats generally avoid the searing heat of the day by spending the sunlit hours under cover, hidden in shady crevices among the rocks, in burrows, or in other shelters. Night is the time when most desert animals are active, and the sand cat is no exception. Only a few of these secretive cats have ever been seen by humans, either in the wild or in zoos.

Another African cat that has sel-

dom been exhibited in zoos and is hardly ever observed in the wild is the black-footed cat (*Felis nigripes*). With a total length of less than a foot and a half, including the tail, it is the smallest of all felines. Tawny with large black spots, the black-footed cat inhabits parts of Botswana, including the Kalahari Desert, and the interior of South Africa. It is nocturnal, hiding during the day in holes or in hollows that have formed in abandoned termite mounds. Its habit of sheltering in insect mounds has led some South Africans to call the creature the "ant hill tiger." Zoologists believe that the black-footed cat feeds on mice and other small rodents, and perhaps on reptiles, which it

Opposite: Adult serval. Below: Young serval. This cat bears its young in the abandoned burrows of other animals such as porcupines. Servals are extremely agile, more so even than many other cats. They roam most of Africa south of the Sahara Desert.

217

Mysterious in the wild, the Asian golden cat, also called Temminck's cat, has been kept in a number of zoos. One captive individual of this species had a life span of seventeen years. When they are kept in the proper environment and are well cared for, cats tend to live longer in captivity than in the wild.

unearths by digging with its powerful forepaws.

The little that is known about the biology of this cat comes from studies of captives. A few black-footed cats have been bred in captivity, so something of their reproductive biology has been revealed. Scientists know, for example, that the female goes into heat for about three days, though she is receptive to the advances of the male for only a fraction of that time. The gestation period is slightly more than two months. Young black-footed cats mature rapidly. They are strong hunters even during their early weeks with their mother.

One of the most adaptable African cats is the serval (*Felis serval*), which has very long legs, a slender build, and a head that seems too small for its body. The serval is a cat of moderate size, almost two feet high at the shoulder, with a short, but not bobbed, tail. The standard color is yellowish with black spots and stripes on the shoulders and back, but there are numerous color variations. There are a few black servals, and one West African variety has a gray-tinged coat and spots that have diminished to speckles. This type is often called the servaline or small-spotted serval. For a long time it was thought to be an entirely different species from the serval, but most scientists now consider it to be merely a color variation. Sometimes serval litters in West Africa have individuals with both normal

speckled markings. The type with the small spots is especially numerous in those parts of West Africa with savannah.

South of the Sahara, the serval is found throughout much of the continent, except for the extreme southern tip. The serval's adaptability is demonstrated by the great variety of habitats in which it flourishes. It inhabits forests, especially those that are not too dense; savannahs, both grassy and desertlike; marshes; and mountains. Where the countryside is very dry, the cat clings to watercourses, but in areas of sufficient rainfall it wanders freely.

Perhaps the serval's most unusual habitat is in Kenya, in the high mountain moorlands of Mount Kenya and the nearby Aberdare range. Some of these mountains are more than 12,000 feet high. The Aberdare moors are especially well known for servals, including black ones. Swept by chill winds and often covered with clouds of cold mist and fog, the moorlands are laced with clear, icy streams, speckled with flowers, and dotted with thickets of giant heath. It is an impressive setting in which to view the serval, especially when the cat travels with great bounds through the low moorland growth.

In tall grass or vegetation the serval leaps high into the air to keep its bearings. Like the caracal, it jumps to catch birds on the wing. Exceptionally agile, the serval also climbs with ease and has been

This jungle cat has killed a victim and is carrying it off to a quiet place where it can eat peacefully. Jungle cats range across Asia to the Nile delta of Egypt, where, thousands of years ago, their genes contributed to the development of the domestic cat.

known to chase tree hyraxes into the branches. (Hyraxes are small animals that resemble rodents but really are closely related to the elephant.) Servals also eat fish, small antelopes, and especially rodents, which they sometimes claw out of their dens. Most of their hunting is done at night.

The female serval's period of heat lasts only a day or two, but it occurs several times a year. The young—between one and three per litter—are born in abandoned burrows of porcupines and other moderate-size animals, and sometimes in rock shelters.

The wet, steaming jungles of central and western Africa, where the African wildcat is not found, are the home of the golden cat (*Felis aurata*). Slightly smaller than the serval, ranging in color from reddish-gold to dark gray, with dark, often conspicuous, spots, this cat resembles a small leopard. Extremely secretive, the golden cat sticks to the deepest forest. Almost nothing is known about its habits other than the fact that, like most of the smaller cats, it often eats rodents and birds.

Along with the African wildcat, the ancient Egyptians sometimes kept a somewhat larger animal, known today as the jungle cat (*Felis chaus*). Despite its name, this cat does not inhabit the jungle in Africa. On this continent, the only place it is found is in the swamps of the Nile delta, hardly much farther south than Cairo.

220

Actually, Africa is only the fringe of the jungle cat's range. It is chiefly Asiatic. Reed beds, marshes, and other wet areas from Asia Minor through the Caspian region to India and Southeast Asia are the main habitat of the jungle cat. However, it occasionally ventures into grasslands. As might befit a cat that was kept in the homes of ancient Egyptians, the jungle cat sometimes takes up residence in abandoned buildings. Powerfully built, with a fairly short tail and large, pointed ears, the jungle cat is a muddy tan color. It hunts mostly in the evenings and mornings, just after sunset and just before sunrise. Its prey is typical of the small cats, except that it is much more likely than other cats to eat frogs, something not unexpected for an animal that inhabits wetlands.

In south-central Asia, where jungle cats have been studied, the species seems to mate between late winter and early spring. Like most of the small cats, including the domestic cat, it has a gestation period of slightly more than two months. Denning in burrows that have been abandoned by other animals, the female jungle cat may bear up to a half-dozen young, though litters are usually smaller than that.

The Asian species of the golden cat, also called Temminck's cat (*Felis temmincki*), is a little larger than its African relative, and also clings to the forest. It has several common color phases, including black and brown. It ranges from Tibet and central China through India and Southeast Asia into Indonesia. The Asian golden cat is quite mysterious, and scientists know very little about its habits in the wild. In its native lands, the cat is regarded with considerable awe, more than might be expected for a cat of only moderate size. It has a number of local names—"golden leopard" in parts of China, "rock cat" in the Himalayas. In Burma it is considered the most noble of all felines. Although the Asian golden cat inhabits dense forests, it seldom ventures into the trees. Roving the forest floor, it stalks rodents, birds, and small deer. Stories about its ferocity abound, and some Asians claim that despite its relatively small size, the cat can tackle prey as large as young wild cattle.

The leopard cat (*Felis bengalensis*) is found from eastern Siberia west to Iran, and south through India and Southeast Asia all the way to the Philippines. Its coloration is rather like the leopard's, except that its dark spots run horizontally and are set almost in rows along the length of the body. Like the big cat after which it is named, the leopard cat varies considerably in size and in the shade of the coat in different parts of its range. The variations have led some scientists to classify the animal into three separate species. Other zoologists consider the variations to be only races, or subspecies of *Felis bengalensis*.

Two leopard cats rest in a quiet corner. This species is small, about the size of a domestic cat, and has a reputation for fierceness. Leopard cats inhabit a vast part of Asia, from eastern Siberia west to Iran and south through India and Southeast Asia to the Philippines.

223

Right: The fishing cat of southern Asia is a picture of feline dignity. It is a strong animal, about the size of the bobcat of North America. It lives largely in tidal areas, where it stalks the sides of creeks and streams, ever ready to snatch up fish in its paws. A young fishing cat is pictured opposite.

In its part of the world, the leopard cat has a reputation for fierceness similar to that of the wildcat in Europe. In zoos, however, leopard cats seem to shed their savagery and become highly manageable. In some parts of their wide range, leopard cats are among the most common mammalian predators. One place where leopard cats are especially numerous is in the basin of the lower Mekong River, in Indochina. Though it has been devastated by decades of warfare, this basin still abounds in the tropical forests that are the ideal habitat for these little cats. Leopard cats are also common near villages, most likely because large numbers of rodents are attracted to the crops and garbage found around human settlements.

Hunting after dark, the leopard cat is the scourge of a wide variety of animals, from small birds to the tiny mouse deer. It also frequently raids farms and villages for poultry. The leopard cat uses a variety of dens to bear its young, including hollow trees, caves, and rock shelters.

Like some of the small felines of South America and Africa, a number of Asian cats are so mysterious that they have been observed by scientists only a few times. As a result, most of their habits are unknown. Among these is the fishing cat (*Felis viverrina*) of southern Asia, found from India to China and south to Java and Taiwan. About the size of a bob-

cat, it is a strong animal, said to kill sheep at times, and it has a reputation for readily taking on any animal that bothers it. As its name indicates, the greater portion of its diet consists of fish, which it snags in the water with its paw. It also feeds on other aquatic animals such as crabs, frogs, and toads, as well as on birds. Not surprisingly, it lives near water. It seems to prefer tidal marshes, mangrove swamps, and deltas.

Two other little-known cats are the two species of marbled cats. One, *Felis marmorata*, looks like a minuscule clouded leopard. Ranging from Nepal and Burma to Borneo, it seems to be highly arboreal, though some zoologists theorize that it hunts mainly on the ground. An unusual trait has been noticed in captive

The rare, seldom-seen marbled cat inhabits jungles both in the lowlands and in the mountains, from the Himalayas south through Burma to Borneo. It is an extremely skillful climber and probably takes much of its prey in the trees.

specimens. When the cat is not moving about, whether it is sitting or standing, it keeps its back in a strongly arched position. The other species, *Felis badia*, is also highly arboreal. Restricted to Borneo, it is sometimes called the red cat. Both species are such adept climbers that they can catch monkeys and birds in the branches.

Almost as small as the black-footed cat of Africa is yet another mysterious and extremely rare Asian species, the flat-headed cat (*Felis planiceps*). It ranges through the Malay peninsula to Sumatra and Borneo. It has a rusty coat covered with a combination of spots and stripes. The flat-headed cat has a rather unusual form, with very small ears and an elongated skull that, as the animal's name implies, is quite compressed. The tail is relatively short and the legs are stubby, indicating that the cat is primarily a ground-dweller. The flat-headed cat's habitat resembles that of the fishing cat—wetlands and flood plains are preferred. It is believed that this cat stalks the water's edge for aquatic animals such as frogs and fish, which it catches with its very large claws.

The rusty-spotted cat (*Felis rubiginosa*) of India and Sri Lanka, another rare species, is about the size of a house cat. It is a denizen of forests and scrubby plains, where it preys on a variety of birds and small mammals. The steppes of western China, especially in Mongolia and in

Variously called the Pallas cat, the steppe cat, and the manul, this creature of the high plateaus and mountains north of India is marvelously adapted to snow and cold. It is believed to be an ancestor of the Persian and other long-haired breeds of domestic cat.

the provinces of Szechwan and Kansu, are the home of the seldom-seen Chinese desert cat (*Felis bieti*). This cat must cope with one of the harshest climates in the world—summers are sizzling hot, winter temperatures fall well below zero, and rough, dry winds sweep across the steppes year-round. The Chinese desert cat, a little larger than a house cat, is yellowish-gray in color and, like the African wildcat, has reddish fur behind the ears.

The area inhabited by the desert cat is the eastern edge of the broad range of the Pallas, or steppe, cat (*Felis manul*), also known as the manul. This species inhabits the high plains of Asia and the surrounding mountains, all the way to the shores of the Caspian Sea. The north-south span of the range is between Siberia and the Himalayas. Much of this area is very high in altitude, and the steppe cat sometimes wanders well above 12,000 feet, where it must adjust to near-arctic conditions. This cat hunts on places like the high plateau country of Tibet, a wind-swept tableland that is one of the most desolate landscapes in the world. The treeless plateau has almost no shrubs, and even grass is a rarity except around waterholes, which are scarce. The only plants that can survive the severe conditions of this region grow very low to the ground and have a hairlike covering that provides insulation.

Even a quick look at the steppe cat reveals that it is extremely well adapted for cold weather. Though it is no taller or longer than a house cat, it is much chunkier, with very short legs and a short muzzle. Short extremities are an advantage for an animal living in an arctic climate, for the warm blood carried by the arteries does not have to travel far from the body to the feet, and thus little heat is lost. Similarly, short ears—and the steppe cat's are tiny—allow only a minimal loss of body heat. Moreover, a bulky body produces more heat than a slender one would.

The steppe cat's yellowish-gray fur is long and thick everywhere but on the top of its back. The longest hair is on the animal's underside. Like short extremities and small ears, the variation in hair length is an important adaptation to the frigid climate in which the cat lives. The thinner coat on the back permits greater absorption of heat from the sun. The extra-long hair covering the belly and tail provides excellent insulation against the cold, snow-covered ground.

The short ears that help the steppe cat cope with the cold are also an advantage for stalking prey in the rugged terrain it inhabits. The cat can hide behind rocks and look out over them without being betrayed by its ears. Furthermore, the steppe cat's eyes are located well up on its head, another advantage for peering over barriers while remaining unseen by the prey.

Like other felines, the steppe cat eats a variety of creatures, especially small mammals. Perhaps the most common prey of this high-mountain cat is a little mammal called the pika. Sometimes called rock conies, pikas resemble ratlike rodents but are related to the rabbits and hares. There are a dozen species, two in North America and ten in Asia. The Asian species are found from the Himalayas north to Siberia, and on the Japanese island of Hokkaido. Pikas are hardy little animals, remarkably well suited to mountain life. They are active year-round and often come out of their burrows in midwinter, particularly when it is sunny.

With its broad face and head and its thick, luxuriant coat, the steppe cat bears a resemblance to two of the most beautiful long-haired domestic breeds, the Persian and the Angora. The area of Persia (now Iran) where these breeds originated is close to the Caspian end of the steppe cat's range, and some people suggest that the steppe cat may have contributed its genes to the domestic breeds' ancestral line. It is doubtful, however, that anyone will ever know for certain whether the relationship really exists.

Prowling the remote expanses of central Asia, coping with some of the earth's most forbidding but also breathtaking environments, and keeping its ways concealed from man's eyes, the steppe cat typifies the mystery and majesty of all the wild cats, both small and big.

229

Where to See the Wild Cats

Parks and Preserves

Wild cats can be found at a number of parks and preserves around the world. The chances of actually seeing them depend on several factors. The first consideration is the type of terrain involved. It is much easier and more convenient to see cats in open country than in, say, jungles or mountainous country. Another important factor is the nature of the cats themselves. A secretive species such as the cougar may abound in a national park or forest, but even experts seldom see it unless it is lured by bait or treed by dogs. Lions, on the other hand, not only live in country that lends itself to easy viewing, but do not seem to mind being watched, even by caravans of tourists in buses.

Because of the open environment, and because lions and cheetahs usually allow themselves to be seen, the savannahs of East Africa and the plains of southern Africa are the best places in the world to observe wild cats, especially big ones, in their native setting. There are also a few places in Asia where wild cats can be seen fairly easily. In most other areas, it takes considerable work and persistence to find the wild cats, and even when they are seen, they may be glimpsed only briefly. The list that follows includes both prime locations for observing cats and areas where, with a bit of effort, travelers may be rewarded with a look at some of nature's most splendid creatures.

Africa

Amboseli National Park, Kenya. This area, formerly a game reserve, has recently been reclassified as a national park. Largely savannah, with occasional mountains and marshes, it covers 1,200 square miles. Lions and cheetahs are readily seen; leopards are somewhat less visible. Servals, wildcats, and a few other small felines also inhabit the area.

Marsabit National Reserve, Kenya. Caracals may be seen in this 800-square-mile reserve located in the desolate northern region of Kenya. Lions, and occasionally leopards, also are on hand.

Masai Mara Game Reserve, Kenya. Covering 700 square miles, with vast rolling savannah cut by small streams and dotted with acacia woods, this preserve is known for its tree-climbing lions. Several of the lions often can be seen at once in the branches of some of the large acacia groves. Cheetahs are also common here.

Nairobi National Park, Kenya. Bordering on Kenya's capital, this wilderness is small—only 44 square miles—but has lion prides, leopards, and cheetahs. African wildcats can be seen prowling at the edges of the city.

Tsavo National Park, Kenya. Covering

more than 8,000 square miles, this huge park contains lions, leopards, and cheetahs, as well as some of the smaller cats.
Kruger National Park, South Africa. More than 7,340 square miles, this vast park has sizable populations of lions, cheetahs, and leopards.
Lake Manyara National Park, Tanzania. Slightly more than 120 square miles, this park of mountains, forest, and plains has tree-climbing lions and many leopards.
Ngorongoro Crater Conservation Area, Tanzania. Within this great volcanic crater are 2,500 square miles of plains that are the home of lions, cheetahs, and a large population of leopards. Servals and wildcats also live here.
Serengeti National Park, Tanzania. More than 5,600 square miles, this is Tanzania's prime national park. It is perhaps the best place in the world to view leopards. Lions and cheetahs abound here as well.

Asia

Corbett National Park, India. This 125-square-mile park, not far from New Delhi, is famed for its tigers.
Kanha National Park, India. Covering 123 square miles of high mountains, meadows, and forest, this park contains tigers, a few leopards, and smaller jungle cats.
Kaziranga National Park, India. Jungle-covered and marshy in many areas, this 166-square-mile park is the home of both tigers and leopards.
National Park and Wildlife Sanctuary, Nepal. Site of the famed Tiger Tops Hotel, this 1,000-square-mile park in the Himalayan foothills is primarily thick jungle and is noted for its tigers and leopards. Tigers are baited for observers in blinds.
Khao Yai National Park, Thailand. Only a two-hour automobile ride from Bangkok, this 800-square-mile park offers cabins, a golf course, and a good chance of seeing tigers. The cats sometimes can be seen on the grassy meadows and hillsides that dot the forested region. The leopard cat is also common in the area, and leopards also are occasionally seen.

South America

Sierra de la Macarena National Park, Colombia. This 1.5-million-acre park, a meeting ground of Amazon jungle and high Andean forest, is the home of both jaguars and ocelots.
Henry Pittier National Park, Venezuela. This large park (225,000 acres) is a relatively short drive from Caracas. Cougars, jaguars, and some of the smaller cats dwell in its jungles, but they may be somewhat difficult to find.

North America

Jasper National Park, Alberta, Canada. 231

Both lynxes and cougars live within this park's more than 2.5 million acres.

Pacific Rim National Park, British Columbia, Canada. This park, which covers almost a million acres, is located on Vancouver Island, site of the provincial capital, Victoria. This is the heart of cougar country, and the cats are truly plentiful in the park.

Mt. McKinley National Park, Alaska, U.S.A. Like many national parks in the northern part of the continent, this preserve of more than 3,000 miles is the home of the lynx. Lynxes can be seen in virtually any park within the range of the snowshoe hare.

Sequoia National Park/King's Canyon National Park, California, U.S.A. Sequoia National Park, more than 600 square miles, and King's Canyon, more than 700 square miles, adjoin one another and so form a single environmental unit. This wilderness is dominated by huge sequoia trees. Bobcats roam the forest here, as do a handful of cougars.

Yosemite National Park, California, U.S.A. Almost 1,200 square miles, Yosemite lies in the high country of California's Sierra Nevada range. Bobcats inhabit the region, and cougars hunt the park's many deer.

Everglades National Park, Florida, U.S.A. This immense region—2,188 square miles of subtropical marshland, prairies, and swampland—is one of the last havens of the Florida race of the cougar. However, the cats are so rare and secretive that they are almost never seen. Bobcats are common in this park.

Yellowstone National Park, Montana-Wyoming, U.S.A. This is the biggest national park in the United States, covering more than 3,470 square miles. It contains many large mammals, including bobcats and cougars, but the cats are seldom seen.

Olympic National Park, Washington, U.S.A. This 1,400-square-mile wilderness in Washington's Olympic Mountains probably offers the best opportunity for seeing cougars in the United States. The cats are abundant in the park's wet conifer forests. Bobcats inhabit the area, too.

Europe

National Park of Abruzzi, Italy. Noted for its wolves and bears, this 112-square-mile wilderness in the mountains south of Rome also supports populations of the European wildcat.

Bialowieza National Forest, Poland. Five hours' drive from Warsaw, this park covers almost 240,000 acres on the border with the Soviet Union. A remnant of Europe's primeval forest, it is famed as the home of a free-living European bison herd. It also has a large lynx population.

Recommended Zoos

The zoos listed below all have better-than-average cat collections. Those marked with an asterisk (*) are noted for breadth of collection, unusual rarities, or high-quality exhibits.

*Arizona-Sonora Desert Museum,
  Tucson, Arizona, U.S.A.
Los Angeles Zoo,
  Los Angeles, California, U.S.A.
*San Diego Zoo,
  San Diego, California, U.S.A.
San Francisco Zoo,
  San Francisco, California, U.S.A.
*Denver Zoo, Denver, Colorado, U.S.A.
*National Zoo, Washington, D.C., U.S.A.
Brookfield Zoo,
  Brookfield, Illinois, U.S.A.
Lincoln Park Zoo,
  Chicago, Illinois, U.S.A.
Topeka Zoo, Topeka, Kansas, U.S.A.
Louisville Zoo,
  Louisville, Kentucky, U.S.A.
*Minnesota State Zoo,
  Apple Valley, Minnesota, U.S.A.
St. Louis Zoo, St. Louis, Missouri, U.S.A.
Albuquerque Zoo,
  Albuquerque, New Mexico, U.S.A.
*Bronx Zoo, Bronx, New York, U.S.A.
Buffalo Zoo, Buffalo, New York, U.S.A.
North Carolina Zoo,
  Asheboro, North Carolina, U.S.A.
*Cincinnati Zoo,
Cincinnati, Ohio, U.S.A.
Cleveland Zoo, Cleveland, Ohio, U.S.A.
Toledo Zoo, Toledo, Ohio, U.S.A.
Oklahoma City Zoo,
  Oklahoma City, Oklahoma, U.S.A.
Portland Zoo, Portland, Oregon, U.S.A.
Philadelphia Zoo,
  Philadelphia, Pennsylvania, U.S.A.
Houston Zoo, Houston, Texas, U.S.A.
*Milwaukee County Zoo,
  Milwaukee, Wisconsin, U.S.A.
Chapultepec Zoo,
  Mexico City, Mexico
Caracas Zoo, Caracas, Venezuela
*Peking Zoo, Peking, China
Ueno Zoo, Tokyo, Japan
Singapore Zoo, Singapore
*Colombo Zoo, Colombo, Sri Lanka
Dusit Zoo, Bangkok, Thailand
Taronga Park Zoo, Sydney, Australia
Vienna Zoo, Vienna, Austria
Prague Zoo, Prague, Czechoslovakia
London Zoo, London, England
Phoenix Park Zoo, Dublin, Ireland
*East Berlin Zoo,
  East Berlin, East Germany
Berlin Zoo, Berlin, West Germany
*Frankfurt Zoo,
  Frankfurt am Main, West Germany
*Rome Zoo, Rome, Italy
*Lodz Zoo, Lodz, Poland
Warsaw Zoo, Warsaw, Poland
*Basel Zoo, Basel, Switzerland

233

Bibliography

Allen, Glover M., *Extinct and Vanishing Mammals of the Western Hemisphere*. New York, American Committee for International Wild Life Protection, 1942.

Blood, Don; Hall, Tom W.; and Baumgarten, Susan, *Rocky Mountain Wildlife*. Vancouver, B. C., Hancock House, 1976.

Carr, William H., *The New Basic Book of the Cat*. New York, Charles Scribner's Sons, 1978.

Chinery, Michael, *Animal Communities*. New York, Franklin Watts, 1972.

Crandall, Lee S., *The Management of Wild Animals in Captivity*. Chicago, The University of Chicago Press, 1964.

Curry-Lindahl, Kai, *Europe: A Natural History*. New York, Random House, 1964.

Harper, Francis, *Extinct and Vanishing Mammals of the Old World*. New York, American Committee for International Wild Life Protection, 1945.

Harrington, Fred A., *A Guide to the Mammals of Iran*. Tehran, Department of the Environment, 1977.

Kurten, Bjorn, *The Age of Mammals*. New York, Columbia University Press, 1972.

McBride, Glen, *Animal Families*. Pleasantville, N.Y., Reader's Digest, 1971.

McDougal, Charles, *The Face of the Tiger*. London, Rivington Books, 1977.

Matthews, L. Harrison, *The Life of Mammals*. New York, Universe Books, 1971.

Osborn, Henry Fairfield, *The Age of Mammals in Europe, Asia, and North America*. New York, Macmillan, 1910.

Palmer, Ralph S., *The Mammal Guide: Mammals of North America North of Mexico*. Garden City, N.Y., Doubleday, 1954.

Rue, Leonard Lee, *Sportsman's Guide to Game Animals*. New York, Harper & Row, 1968.

Schaller, George B., *The Deer and the Tiger: A Study of Wildlife in India*. Chicago, The University of Chicago Press, 1967.

———, *The Serengeti Lion: A Study in Predator-Prey Relations*. Wildlife Behavior and Ecology Series. Chicago, The University of Chicago Press, 1972.

Smith, F. V., *Purpose in Animal Behavior*. London, Hutchinson, 1971.

Teer, James G., and Swank, Wendell G., *The Status of the Leopard in Africa South of the Sahara*. Washington, D.C., Office of Endangered Species, U.S. Fish and Wildlife Service, 1977.

van der Woude, R., et al., *Animals in Danger*. Strasbourg, Council of Europe, 1969.

Walker, Ernest P., et al., *Mammals of the World*, 3rd ed. 2 vols. Baltimore, The Johns Hopkins Press, 1975.

Picture Credits

BC—Bruce Coleman, Inc.
TO—Tierbilder Okapia
TS—Tom Stack & Associates

half title: lion, F. S. Mitchell, TS.
title page: Indian tiger, G. D. Plage, BC.
contents: cougar, Erwin A. Bauer.
page 239: bobcat, Stouffer Productions Ltd.,
Animals Animals

Introduction
8: George Schaller. 10-11: S. Paul. 12: Erwin A. Bauer

1. The Wild Cats: Their Origins
14-15: American Museum of Natural History. 17: N.Y. Public Library. 18: American Museum of Natural History. 19: University Museum, Philadelphia. 21: (both) Library of Congress. 22: Earl Kubis, TS. 24: M. P. Kahl. 27: Warren Garst, TS. 29: Leonard Lee Rue III, TS. 30: M. P. Kahl. 31: A. B. Thomas, Animals Animals. 32: Lovell M. Groves, Outdoor Photographers League. 33: Gary Milburn, TS. 35: Anthony Mercieca. 36: Robert Burr Smith. 37: Bunge, TO. 39: F. Peter, Jacana. 40: Leonard Lee Rue III.

2. The Wild Cats and Their Land
42-43: George Schaller. 45: Wolfgang Bayer, BC. 47: Bob Campbell, BC. 48-49: Shyla Gotlieb, Outdoor Photographers League. 50-51: Robert Burr Smith. 53: Leonard Lee Rue III. 55: Erwin A. Bauer. 56: J. P. Ferrero. 58-59: S. Paul. 60-61: Burton McNeely. 62, 63: C. A. Morgan. 64-65: George Schaller. 66: (top) Marvin Newman, Woodfin Camp; (btm) Dr. G. J. Chafaris. 67: Tom Nebbia, Woodfin Camp. 68-69: George Schaller. 70-71: Tom Nebbia, Woodfin Camp. 73: J. Allan Cash Ltd. 74: Joe McDonald, TS. 75: Clem Haagner, BC. 76-77: George Schaller, BC. 78: Kenneth W. Fink. 79: G. D. Dodge & D. R. Thompson, BC. 82: Jane Burton, BC. 83: BC. 84: Clem Haagner, BC.

3. The Hunters
86-87: Tom Brakefield. 89: Leonard Lee Rue III. 90-91: George Schaller. 92-93: Leonard Lee Rue III, TS. 94: David C. Fritts, Animals Animals. 95: Fran Allan, Animals Animals. 96: Warren Garst, TS. 97: A. Root, TO. 98: Leonard Lee Rue III, TS. 99: Eugene Moll, TO. 100-101: Marvin Newman, Woodfin Camp. 102-103: Tom Nebbia. 104: N. Myers, BC. 106-107, 109: George Schaller. 110-111: Gary Milburn, TS. 113: (both) A. Root, TO. 114: Leonard Lee Rue III. 115: Robert Burr Smith. 116-117: Stouffer Productions Ltd., Animals Animals. 118-119: BC. 120: Tom Brakefield, TS.

4. The Young Cats
122-123: M. P. Kahl. 125: Erik Parbst, Black Star. 126, 127: Fran Allan, Animals Animals. 128: M. P. Kahl. 129: A. Root, TO. 130: Tom Nebbia. 131: (top) Audrey Ross; (btm) M. P. Kahl. 132-133: Scottland Photo Studio. 134-135: Warren & Genny Garst, TS. 136: Gerald Cubitt. 137: Tom Brakefield. 138-139: Wolfgang & Candy Bayer, BC. 140: M. P. Kahl. 141: Warren Garst, TS. 142: TO. 143: M. Freeman, BC. 144-145: J. P. Ferrero. 147: S. Paul. 149: San Diego Zoo. 150: Robert Zappalorti. 151: Warren Garst, TS. 152: (top) Warren Garst, TS; (btm) Leonard Lee Rue III. 155: (top) Leonard Lee Rue III, Animals Animals; (btm) Robert Burr Smith. 156: Al Nelson, TS.

5. Life Among the Wild Cats
158-159: Marvin Newman, Woodfin Camp. 161, 162: (all) A. Root, TO. 163: George Schaller. 164-165: Rajesh Bedi. 166, 167: (all) M. P. Kahl. 168, 169: Leonard Lee Rue III. 170: Peter Johnson. 171: A. Root, TO. 172-173: Jeff Foott, BC. 174: Marvin Newman, Woodfin Camp. 176-177: George Schaller. 179: (top) BC; (btm) Agence Hoa-Qui. 180-181: M. Amin, BC. 182: J. P. Ferrero. 183: Naresh & Rajesh Bedi. 184: Rajesh Bedi. 185: S. Paul. 186: J. P. Ferrero. 187: Jean-Philippe Varin, Jacana. 188: S. Paul. 189: Sankhala, TO. 190-191: Schmidecker, TO. 193: Ken Stinnett, TS. 194: (top) Tom Brakefield; (btm) TO. 195: Tom Brakefield. 196: Warren Garst, TS.

6. The Smaller Kin
198-199: Warren Garst, TS. 201: Diana & Rick Sullivan, BC. 202: Jeff Foott, BC. 203: Marilyn K. Krog. 204: Arthur Bertrand, Jacana. 207: TO. 208: Hans Reinhard, BC. 209: Jane Burton, BC. 211: (top) Lynn Stone, BC; (btm) TO. 212: BC. 214-215: N.Y. Zoological Society. 216: Marilyn K. Krog. 217: Edward Ross. 219: BC. 220-221, 222: J. P. Ferrero. 224: Gary Milburn, TS. 225: TO. 226-227: BC. 228: N.Y. Zoological Society.

Index